The Sacraments Today

A THEOLOGY FOR ARTISANS OF A NEW HUMANITY

Volumes 1-3 & 5

The Community Called Church

Grace and the Human Condition

Our Idea of God

Evolution and Guilt

ORBIS  BOOKS

VOLUME FOUR

The Sacraments Today

BY JUAN LUIS SEGUNDO, S.J., IN COLLABORATION
WITH THE STAFF OF THE PETER FABER CENTER
IN MONTEVIDEO, URUGUAY
TRANSLATED BY JOHN DRURY

MARYKNOLL, NEW YORK

Abbreviations Used in This Volume

AA *Apostolicam actuositatem.* Vatican II. Decree on the Apostolate of the Laity. November 18, 1965.

Denz. Denzinger-Schönmetzer, *Enchiridion Symbolorum.* Fribourg: Herder, 1963.

GS *Gaudium et spes.* Vatican II. Pastoral Constitution on the Church in the Modern World, December 7, 1965.

MED Second General Conference of Latin American Bishops (Medellin, Colombia, 1968). Official English edition edited by Louis Michael Colonnese, Latin American Division of United States Catholic Conference, Washington, D.C.: *The Church in the Present-Day Transformation of Latin America in the Light of the Council;* Vol. I, Position Papers; Vol. II, Conclusions.

SC *Sacrosanctum Concilium.* Vatican II. Constitution on the Sacred Liturgy. December 4, 1963.

Biblical citations are taken from The New English Bible, with the Apocrypha (New York and London: Oxford University Press and Cambridge University Press, 1970).

Citations of conciliar documents, unless otherwise indicated, are taken from Walter M. Abbot, S.J. (ed). *The Documents of Vatican II* (New York: Guild-America-Association, 1966).

Wherever possible, other church and papal documents are cited on the basis of translations in *The Pope Speaks* Magazine (Washington, D.C.).

ORIGINALLY PUBLISHED BY EDICIONES CARLOS LOHLÉ, BUENOS AIRES, © 1971.

COPYRIGHT © 1974, ORBIS BOOKS, MARYKNOLL, NEW YORK 10545

LIBRARY OF CONGRESS CATALOG CARD NUMBER: 73-77359

ISBN SERIES   088344-480-1 VOLUME 088344-484-4
PAPER: SERIES 088344-486-0 VOLUME 088344-490-9

MANUFACTURED IN THE UNITED STATES OF AMERICA

SECOND PRINTING 1975

VOLUME FOUR

Contents

The Sacraments Today

INTRODUCTION

A New Crisis for the Sacraments?

The fact that the sacramental life of the Church has entered a crisis in recent years is no secret to anyone. Any sociologist can verify it, and every priest is experiencing it. The scarcity of priestly vocations is itself one more symptom of this crisis, for the priest is "the man of the sacraments."

What may not be so clearly perceived is the original aspect of the crisis through which we are living. The sacramental life of the Church has gone into decline at different points in church history. But the decline we are now witnessing has a distinctive feature that makes it not only new but unique. It has not been brought on by ignorance, indifference, or rebellion against the Church. Difficult as it may be to believe at first glance, *it has been brought on by the Church itself*.

Section I

Let us consider two examples. No one can deny that over the last century, specifically in countries with a Christian majority, the traditional procession on the feast of Corpus Christi has—perhaps imperceptibly—taken on a triumphalist character. And to speak of triumphalism is to speak of aggressiveness, latent aggressiveness at the very least. Without fully realizing it, people set value on the imposing presence of crowds of Christians in the streets. They saw and prized the victory over human respect which this presence represented. For it in turn extorted respect and external signs of deference even from those nonbelievers who watched the passing Eucharist.

Now it is undeniable that many Catholics today instinctively feel, or consciously maintain, that there is something improper and wrongheaded about the above outlook that has surrounded the celebration of Corpus Christi. If we investigate a bit to find the reasons behind this uneasiness, we will have no trouble in reaching one conclusion: the reform of the liturgy, despite its timidity, has exerted no small influ-

3

ence on the new attitude by the very fact that it has made the basic texts surrounding the Eucharist comprehensible in the vernacular language.

Extricated from their almost magical context, the very words of institution tell us that we are dealing with an action designed to carry meaning and significance. And to speak of such signification is to speak of dialogue.

Now obviously enough the Eucharist transmits signification *to the faithful*: i.e., to those who plumb its meaning through faith. So of itself the Eucharist does not dialogue with those who do not have faith. It is senseless to carry it around like a banner, seeking to win a victory thereby. For such a "victory" has no meaning. The only victory the Eucharist can win is within the Christian community: it can be converted into an element of dialogue concerning the very same human problems that harass all human beings. In other words, the Eucharist is not a sign for the world; rather, it is a sign for the Christian community which seeks to be at the service of the world and thus to be itself a sign.

So it would appear that it is relatively easy for us to explain the reason behind the negative reaction of many Christians—including some of the best—to what we might call a fallacious use of the Eucharist.

But, alas, the crisis is running way ahead of our explanation, leaving us and our reasoning in a cloud of dust. Taking off from a particular use of the Eucharist, it is moving in on the Eucharist itself. Here again, it is not without reason—or reasons.

The Eucharist is a sign—an efficacious sign by virtue of the grace it confers—of what the Christian community ought to be. Now if it is that in fact, would it not be possible for us to move directly to that ideal?

Let us consider this question. The ideal in question could be none other than love. The Eucharist signifies to us, and confers on us, the possibility of loving each other and of transforming this love into an impetus and a message for the entire human community. Now if we are talking about a community of adults, would it not be possible for such a community to attain this goal without going through an invariable ritual act that is all too familiar?

Let us take a look at the four Gospels. Clearly the Gospel of John is the one that delves most thoroughly into the theme of the Eucharist, both explicitly and implicitly. But what do we find when his Gospel comes to narrate the last supper of Jesus with his disciples? We find that while the three Synoptic Gospels narrate the story of the institution of the Eucharist, John's Gospel does not even mention this part of the story. By the same token, John's Gospel is the only one that presents another event, introducing it with a solemn prologue and ending it with a solemn epilogue. It tells how Jesus washed the feet of his friends on his last night with them. And it concludes the story with these words of Jesus: "I have set you an example. You are to do as I have done for you" (John 13:15). Furthermore, we know that John saw in this action the love of God being shown to its full extent (*cf.* John 13:1).

What explanation can there be for this extraordinary fact? For John's omission of such a familiar and favorite theme? For his substitution?

The most plausible explanation offered by exegetes is this: where the three Synoptic Gospels narrate the *institution of the sacrament of the Eucharist*, there John narrates *its fulfillment and realization*. Love shown to the full extent within Jesus' community: is that not simultaneously the significance toward which the Eucharist points and the grace that it confers? And is it not to be expected that the image presented by John is much more appealing than that of a ritual gesture—particularly when that gesture today is devoid of the qualities we find expressed in a real human gesture of commitment?

At first glance there would seem to be only one valid objection to this preference: namely, that God really made the possibility of exercising such love conditional upon the sacramental practice. But wouldn't that come down to binding God to canon law? Could God possibly deny to a sincere person the possibility of loving and giving his life to the community and society, just because that person was not in the know about the structure of the Church? Is it possible that the Church is not an aid to man, but rather a restrictive condition with respect to love, grace, and salvation?

With this first example we run into many of the elements that go to make up the new, special, unique sacramental crisis we are now living through. And all the reasons behind the crisis come from church renewal itself. From there we get the liturgical reform, which made the sacramental rites comprehensible. From there we get the idea of a Church whose whole existence is meant to serve the world in a process of dialogue (GS 40; GS 3). From there we get a picture of the sacraments functioning for the sake of the community, rather than the reverse. Finally, insofar as we glimpse the vast, unexpected, and effective pathways of grace, we cannot imagine God offering grace only to those who submit to a determined rite.

Each one of these elements of the Christian life is supported by conciliar texts and by the very life of the Church today. One cannot ignore or deny this fact.

But let us move on to our second example. For years and years, parents have brought their children, while still babies, to the baptismal font. They went through a ceremony which, aside from the external trappings, differed little from the enrollment of the child in the civil register. Only, in the case of baptism, the child was being enrolled in an ecclesiastical register.

Today there are no secrets to the baptismal ceremony. The words and actions of the priest—now understood at last—lead to fundamental and total changes in the life of the child, as far as the eyes of faith can see at least.

Perhaps the expectation was that this unveiling of the mysterious rite would attract people who formerly felt no interest in the sacramental rite because they could not understand it. But in reality something else has happened. While average parents may still continue to bring their children to baptism as much as before, many have come to discover directly and at close range with their own eyes that the baptism of children was a magical rite. It is not just a logical but a sensible discovery.

For the first time in centuries, perhaps, young married Christians are asking themselves whether they really should baptize their babies or not. Their question is sincere, and it is not rare that they give a "no" answer to it. This is a sociological fact that can be readily verified, and it is highly significant.

For the Church it is a serious problem as well. It has itself solemnly and officially proclaimed: "A more critical ability to distinguish religion from *a magical view of the world* and from the superstitions which still circulate purifies religion and exacts day by day a more personal and explicit adherence to faith" (GS 7; our italics). But it is precisely this sort of adherence that is not evident in the baptism of small children. So if baptism is conferred in this way, how can it help but presuppose and imply "a magical view of the world"?

Magical actions are different from ordinary actions in two respects, insofar as their outcome is concerned. Firstly, in terms of expected efficacy, there is no normal relationship between the means employed and the outcome. Secondly, the outcome is not dependent on whim; it is tied by a superhuman power to certain fixed ritual gestures or words.

Now let us look at baptism. When the minister of this sacrament says, "Depart, unclean spirit, from this child!" are we supposed to believe that it does? If the answer is yes, then how can we help but attribute magical power to the words, since there is no real proportion between them and the result they proclaim? If the answer is no, then why not wait until later, until liberty and faith—the works of grace—eventually bring about what the sign points toward?

As the reader can now see, it is those Christians who are more reflective, logical, and interested who are feeling the sacramental crisis to which we have been alluding.

Section II

Let us move on from these two examples to a more global view of the Church in terms of its structures. Readers of the previous volumes in this series will immediately grasp what we are alluding to in the brief summary that follows.

1. The Church was not instituted for the exclusive or particular benefit of those who are within it. It is not an absolute in the plan of God, at least not insofar as it is a visible, historical institution. Indeed it is not even a direct means of salvation independently of the non-Christian world that surrounds it. The Church is sent to that world; and it has worth and salvific impact to the extent that it fulfills this mission, effectively inserting itself into a love that is already existing, operative, and supernatural.

The very nature of the Church's mission is that it must plunge itself into this love that builds up humanity in history. For in every age and place this love runs into new problems, problems that are raised by the solutions found for old problems. History does not stand still. To this moving, changing history God turns with his word, through a living community that must translate this word in terms of the "signs of the times." The latter are the indispensable signs for human dialogue.

Hence interpretation of the signs of the times does not allow the Church to sit back and luxuriate in readymade answers. Such anwers would not be answers at all. The terrain of dialogue would have disappeared. And the word of God, directed to man, would be silenced by the immobilism of the very Church that was founded to transmit it.

Now one need only take a quick glance at the reality of the Church to see in it, at least today, two main features or aspects of its activity. The first main feature has been highlighted more clearly in recent times. It comprises everything that varies and changes in the normal activity of the Church so that the latter can respond in an effective and original way to new problems.

Take the Sunday Mass, for example. We know that efforts have been made, particularly in recent years, to see to it that the commentary on the principal scriptural texts (i.e., the Epistle and the Gospel, which have been fixed for centuries) does enter into real-life dialogue with "the joys and the hopes, the griefs and the anxieties" of contemporary man.

The rest of the Mass, however, is immutable. It is the same in under-developed countries and affluent nations, in residential suburbs and

inner cities, in socialist countries and capitalist countries, in dictatorships
and democracies, in prison chapels and tourist waystations. The rest
of the sacraments evince this second feature, immutability, even more
clearly. Immutability marks a large part, if not the major part, of the
Church's activity.

True enough, the priest does usually devote a part of his time to
dialoguing, counselling, and teaching. He tries to animate Christian communities or groups that are seriously interested in the problems they
share with their fellow men. But one fact is singular and significant:
in most cases his material subsistence depends not on the variable,
dialogue-centered part of his functions, but rather on the invariable,
repetitive, nondialogic part.

Let us try to ponder this reality from the viewpoint of an outsider.
If something remains invariable throughout history, if it is not sensitive
to the changing problems that arise in the progressive construction of
the earth, then only by magic can it be the leaven of this history and
this construction process whose fluctuations and changes it does not
experience.

If that is not the case, then the efficacy of the sacraments has to
do with something that is essentially independent of history. They are
an anachronistic survival from an age when many people viewed the
Church as a perfect society pointing the way toward salvation, equipped
with its own specific means—as specific to it as its own aim and goal,
and dwelling in the midst of a human society pointed toward another
goal.

This view was discarded by Vatican II. But it was rejected long before
that Council—by Christ himself. Let us consider two key Gospel passages
that deal with this matter.

The first is the saying of Jesus recorded by Matthew: "If, when you
are bringing your gift to the altar, you suddenly remember that your
brother has a grievance against you, leave your gift where it is before
the altar. First go and make your peace with your brother" (Matt. 5:
23–24). Our mistake has been in thinking that this reconciliation could
be accomplished in five minutes. But when we realize that the grievance
of two-thirds of mankind against the other one-third is the fact of not
being able to satisfy their hunger, we may well ask ourselves: Will a
five-minute interruption in our sacramental life be enough to reconcile
us? Will a whole lifetime be enough?

We are paying the price for our pagan insistence on the altar. Then
there came a moment when many Christians, perhaps the best of them,
took Jesus' words seriously. We cannot grumble about that: "The Church
also realizes that in working out her relationship with the world she

clearly has great need of the ripening which comes with the experience of the centuries" (GS 43). And ripening presupposes crisis.

The other passage that ought to have been taken seriously by many Christians—those who read the Bible—is also from the Gospel. The enemies of Jesus ask him for a "sign from heaven" (Mark 8:11–13; Matt. 16:1–4 and 12:38–42; Luke 11:16, 29–32 and 12:54–56).

What they are really asking for—these people whom Jesus calls "hypocrites"—is a datum or deed that belongs unmistakably to another realm, that has no trace of ambiguity or temporality in it. They want an aseptic, celestial, supernatural sign—which is nevertheless accessible.

Jesus refuses their request, but he does not refuse to give them a sign. Indeed he often gives them something else, liberating people from their most evident bonds: blindness, deafness, paralysis, despair! But here he refers them back from heaven to earth, where man plays out his liberty and life in the face of ever new and changing signs of the times. He is careful to point out how to go about this uniquely salvific task of interpretation: one must be attentive to the variable, changing element and not be led astray by any apparent or superficial identicalness. "In the evening you say, 'It will be fine weather, for the sky is red'; and in the morning you say, 'It will be stormy today—the sky is red and lowering.' You know how to interpret the appearance of the sky; can you not interpret the signs of the times?"

Earth and time are complex, ambiguous realities. What is seemingly the same thing may signify very different or even opposite things, depending on the place and moment in which we encounter it.

So we find Jesus refusing to give invariable, extraterrestrial signs and referring his listeners back to the interpretation of the variable and the temporal. Is he not thereby telling his Church that, of these two features we have been discussing, only the interpretation of the signs of the times is authentic? Doesn't it mean that the sacraments, as they are lived today, are invariable, aseptic, deceitful signs of a celestial grace that does not enter history?[1]

2. In order to make its own specific and divine contribution to universal salvation, the visible Church *qua* community must be a sign: a sign of the universal salvific plan, of the recapitulation for which the whole universe is waiting, of a message that God sends through his Church in order to contribute toward solutions of man's historical problems that are truly human.

Now here again we find two main features in the life of the Church. On the one hand, it is only in a communitarian way that the Church can effectively translate and "signify" the word of God. No member of the Church, not even its hierarchy—perhaps it less than anyone—pos-

sesses readymade solutions for the problems of history. And even if
someone did possess such solutions, the Church itself would not be
a sign without engaging in the work of making all its members sharers
in the supposed solutions.

Clearly enough the Church is not an army or a political party. But
since it is destined to be a sign, neither can it be a mere juxtaposition
of persons who say, think, and do things that are completely different
or even opposed to each other.

The signification of the Church does not depend on some sort of
impersonal unanimity, to be sure. But it does depend on a communitarian
activity that points toward unity.

On the other side of the coin, however, anyone can see that our
sacramental life embodies a different feature that is poles apart from
the communitarian aspect: it centers around the individual.

The first thing that is evident from the sociology, mentality, and
liturgical context of the average parish is that all the sacraments are
received individually (even if within a celebration attended by many
people). Baptism, confirmation, penance, matrimony, and the anointing
of the sick are given to specific persons—not to the Christian community.
Even when the decision is made to make some of them communal celebrations, everyone considers the sacrament and its effects as relating to
the individual.

Perhaps the clearest case of all is the Eucharist—the communitarian
sacrament *par excellence*. In the celebrations with which we are familiar,
the Eucharist brings people next to each other; it juxtaposes them. It
does not make a community out of the participants. *Each person* "goes
to communion," we say, failing to notice the contradiction in terms.
And from a sociological viewpoint this is undoubtedly the case. Each
individual approaches the sacrament, surrounded by people who are
more or less strangers to him and who will continue to be so after
"communion." The act and fact of receiving communion does not unite
people, reveal them to each other, or forge mutual involvement.

This fact is more important than it may appear to be. We are not
dealing merely with a liturgical defect that the liturgy itself could correct.
We are faced with a much deeper problem: sociologically speaking, it
is the sacramental life of the Church which itself allows people to call
themselves Christians even when nothing unites them with each other.
They can call themselves Christians even though they may think that
another person's way of acting is criminal. The only things that
"commune" in the sacramental realm are attitudes which would shatter
any serious effort at discussion or reunion, and which certainly cause
any group of human beings so constituted to lose any and all specific
import or signification.

Here again we must ask ourselves how we can avoid taking seriously the words of Jesus: "Where two or three have met together in my name, I am there among them" (Matt. 18:20). But if we do take them seriously, we are faced with another important question: When is it that human beings are honestly and truly gathered together in unity? Is it when they are searching for the significance of the gospel in their own lives, and are disposed to pass critical judgment on the latter in order to provide an opening for the former? Or is it when sacramental practice joins people together who share no vital idea of life despite their lip service to Jesus? Who really are the ones gathered together *in his name*?

What has been said so far does not claim to end our discussion of the sacraments. That might just as well be said here, lest any doubts remain. But it is meant to be an honest look at the sacramental crisis through which we are now living. It is an attempt to discover what constitutes both its inner depth and its hopefulness.

It is the most Christian of Christians who is responsible for this crisis. It is the very Spirit of Christ, living in his Church, who has brought it on.[2] Without doubt that same Spirit will fashion a deeper, purer, and more youthful Church in and through this crisis.

NOTES TO INTRODUCTION

1. Consider the dialogue of Jesus with the Samaritan woman (John 4). Does it not seem to promise something else? And also consider what the Epistle to the Hebrews says about grace. Is not grace fully given already, without man having to repeatedly approach some rite in order to receive it?

2. Hence we totally disagree with Cardinal Danièlou's attempt to minimize this crisis by reducing it to a loss of Christian sensibility: "Above all there is the fact that the sense of God is in crisis within the Christian world itself. Our grandmothers came to confession and accused themselves principally of failings in their religious duties. A good person would come in and confess that he had not gone to Sunday Mass and that he had eaten meat on Friday. Today it is just the opposite. Young people confess sins against charity. If you ask them whether they have gone to Sunday Mass, they reply that they may have missed five or six times. It seems a small matter to them. The danger today is the crisis confronting our sense of God, of worship, of prayer . . . " (*Le Monde*, November 28, 1968).

CLARIFICATIONS

I. THE SACRAMENTAL CRISIS AND DESACRALIZATION

In the preceding pages we were talking about a new type of crisis affecting the sacraments. We said that it is not due to indifference toward the Christian faith; that it has in fact developed out of the inner exigencies of the faith.

But if we cast a glance at contemporary social processes, we will find ourselves faced with another question. And this time around we cannot be so sure ahead of time that we will be able to offer the same response. The question is: Is there room for sacraments in a world that is desacralized or that is, at the very least, moving in that direction?[1]

As we have already pointed out, from a sociological point of view the sacraments are seen as religious rites. So true is this that when most theologians try to explain the Christian sacraments, they begin by describing the rites of the various religions which antedated Christianity. In doing this they admit that the first and primary thing is, for them, the similarity. Then they go on to establish the difference between the pagan rites and the Christian sacraments, maintaining that despite the external similarities Christ spiritualized the sacraments. As they see it, even though the gestures and actions seem quite similar, in Christianity they have lost their magical character and have been turned into spiritual realities on another plane entirely.[2] But this explanation does not satisfy us. For however spiritual or material they might be, the sacraments would still continue to be religious instruments bound up with that sphere and endowed with a special power to work some specific sacred effect and achieve some specific sacred aim.

Any sociological study would place the sacraments, as religious actions, at the center of those elements which form the most obvious bridge between Christianity and other religions. So we can say that the sacraments, as they are usually lived, are among the most "religious" elements of real-life Christianity and hence among those elements most vulnerable to the general process of desacralization.

Insofar as they are popular cultic expressions, the sacraments are unavoidably tied up with that particular conception of the religious which is based on the notion of its being separate and apart from the daily reality of the secular and profane world. The very basis of liturgy and sacrament is said to reside in the fact that such separation seems to be essential for an encounter with God.

To make sure we confront the full dimensions of this difficulty, let us add right here that the sacraments are, and can never cease to be, cultic expressions that are not of the everyday variety. In other words, we cannot solve the problem by trying to eliminate external ceremony from the sacraments entirely. The external ceremony can be changed, purified, simplified, and modernized; but there must always be something cultic and ceremonial in the sacraments. They must have their own proper *form*, for without it they would inevitably be confused and identified with other things and would no longer be tangible *signs*. There must be some gesture, some action, some silence that is added to the thing itself and that is an essential component of its special signification. Only in this way can the sign be distinguished from the common, everyday thing itself. Suppose, for example, that we wanted to make the Eucharist look like the family meal of every day and tried to inject "naturalness" into it. If we ended up by passing it around like any piece of bread and eating it with our hamburger while we engaged in a typical everyday conversation, then we would obviously have abolished the sacrament of the Eucharist. Likewise, if we turned baptism into a baby bath and washed the child's hair at the same time, it is not just the Sacred Congregation of Rites that could rightfully complain that this is not the sacrament of baptism. In other words, there must always be some formal requirement in the sacraments because they are signs. So we cannot resolve the present sacramental problem by eliminating the element of form.

The problem here is not simply one of strategy, of modernizing, adapting, and reforming the sacraments so that they pass almost unnoticed and are therefore accepted by the desacralized Christian of today. What we must do is show that the sacraments form part of the very essence of authentic Christian existence.

The process of secularization is a positive achievement for man only when he does not replace one evasion with another. Vatican II does make this pointed remark: "A more critical ability to distinguish religion from a magical view of the world and from the superstitions which still circulate purifies religion." (GS 7). But it also stresses that the process of secularization which it values is one that is *critical*, not one that replaces magic with mere disinterest concerning the deepest question of human existence.

But perhaps the most interesting aspect of the conciliar text cited above is an implicit one. In admitting the benefit that a critical process of secularization can have for Christianity, it is implicitly acknowledging that the present manner of living the Christian religion has need of such a critical process. In other words, it is admitting what must be admitted: i.e., that in actual practice a magic-oriented tendency has taken over a large part of sacramental life.

How did it happen that Christianity took a step backward into the religious realm and fell back into the pagan notion of sacraments as religious instruments? There is a plausible historical explanation for this. The primitive Christian communities confronted the pagan world and found themselves accused of being "atheists." It is a strange accusation, but an understandable one. Christians were considered atheists by the pagans because they did not perform sacrifices or make offerings to any God; hence, as far as pagans were concerned, Christians had no God. (In passing we see from this fact to what extent the Christian sacraments were not lived as religious instruments at first.) Confronted with this accusation Christians, desiring not to be taken as atheists, took pains to transform what Christ had instituted as "gesture" and "sign" into "sacrifice" and "offering."

Quite apart from the influence that this historical situation could have had on the process, it is certain that religion remains a permanent temptation for man. And from the very start Christian revelation was proposed to men who were responsive to a religious conception. And the fact is, as we have already pointed out, that the sacraments were the elements most susceptible of being sacralized, instrumentalized, and turned once again into religious tools.

Sooner or later every separation between the sacred and the profane leads to magic. Why? Because in separating the two realms, it is the realm of the sacred that is given value. And to attain this realm with its value one logically establishes means that have no weight in the realm of the profane. For in the latter realm, as John the Evangelist points out, the only valid and effective love is that which operates in deed and in truth rather than in word and intention.

As we shall see more clearly in Chapter I of this volume, Christ initiates a new liturgy that goes way beyond the sacred and the profane. For, in sanctifying what he has assumed in the Incarnation, Christ turns the very history of man into liturgy. Christ restores to human history its real vocation: i.e., to be the liturgy of the cosmos. And when we say that every Christian is a priest, we mean to signify the sacerdotal vocation of the Christian *to turn his own life into a cultic oblation*.

The priesthood of the new law is Christ's, and only his sacrifice in history is salvific. So it is absolutely essential that those human beings who are chosen, by vocation, to cooperate in the work of saving the world in a sacerdotal way become Christs in turn and enter into his sacrifice in a real way. Well, the point here is that Christian initiation through the sacraments—baptism, confirmation, and the Eucharist— truly realizes this mystery of participation in a conscious, deliberate, and explicit way. The ultimate result of this initiation is that the sacrament of Christ the priest is *the very person of the Christian with all his life and existence*.

This gives special realism to the term "sacramental," because in it is packed the concrete reality of each and every Christian's life. Thus this term should not be taken solely in the post-Tridentine sense of seven efficacious rites. It should also be taken to mean that the People of God itself, as an ecclesial community, is transformed into a sacrament. In other words: there is a visible community of human beings living in real-life contact with the rest of mankind that, through its existential actions, contains, manifests, and communicates the saving presence of Christ.

This "sacramentality" implies that the common priesthood of the faithful should lead them to adopt an attitude that goes far beyond any "ritualism" or "moralism." Instead of enticing them to devotions and religious practices, it will drive them to dedicate themselves to the work of being a true and efficacious sign of salvation—the latter being a far more demanding and vital task.

To talk about a sacramental crisis today, in other words, means to face up to the process of secularization in a positive way. And in the concrete this will call into question any and all "sacramentality" that is detached from the sacramentality of the entire Christian community (LG 1; SC 5; etc.). Only by shouldering their function in this reality, or this effort, will the sacraments get beyond the crisis posed by the process of secularization.

II. THE SACRAMENTAL CRISIS AND THE YOUNGER GENERATION

The crisis we have been describing is reflected, in a much more concrete and informative way, in a recent poll.[3] Taking due account of significant differences between generations, this poll tried to find out whether the respondents perceived any conflict between the Christianity they had been taught in childhood or early adolescence and their present experiences. The latter factor was the atmosphere of the university in the case of students, and the realm of work and family life in the case of those already engaged in a professional career.

They were also asked questions about their conception of Christianity. Is it a good news that brings fulfillment or merely an instrument for achieving one's personal salvation? What do you think about the risk of engaging in personal reflection on the faith? Is this a task only for theologians, or is it a task for each and every Christian even though there is a danger of making a mistake? Isn't it better to accept what the Church proposes without arguing?

With respect to the moral life, the poll tried to find out to what extent the respondents saw it as a complex of external norms imposed on a passive human being, or as a liberty that creates and fulfills a human project.

Only at the end were they asked about the sacramental life and the difficulties they were experiencing in this area. They were asked especially about their reception of the Eucharist and their practice of penance.

Now even though the words "religious" and "sacred" did not appear in the questionnaire, it is obvious that the questions tried to detect elements specific to a "religious" outlook: i.e., a magical conception of dogma, of the moral law, and in the last instance, of the sacraments.[4] The respondent was also given a chance to expatiate on any possible conflict between the Christianity he or she had received and accepted earlier and their present real-life existence: that is, between earlier formulations connected with a "religious" conception and the questions now posed by life in a desacralized world.

What were the results of this poll in broad outline? We can distinguish two groups of responses. In both groups we find the respondents alluding to some type of *conversion* that permitted them to get beyond what they had been taught "in childhood" or "in the catechism" and to arrive at what they called a "more authentic" Christianity. But the Christians in the first group, students for the most part, give the impression that right now they are not experiencing any kind of conflict in the realm of faith and dogma, their conception of the moral law, or their sacramental life; those in the second group on the other hand, people already engaged in their professional career for the most part, are experiencing a much more complex situation. At an earlier date they had gone through the first conversion mentioned above, usually through their participation in some youthful branch of Catholic Action (YCW, for example). But all that *had turned into a problem* once they left the university environment and became a part of real-life society through their professional work. In some cases they looked back nostalgically to the way they had lived the faith in their student days, With greater or lesser clarity they saw a conflict between what it meant to them then and what it meant to them now. In short, they bore clear witness to the fact that they were going through a crisis in all three realms: dogma, moral principles, and sacramental life.

Before we analyze these responses in detail, we want the reader to *sense* and *feel* the difference between the positions of the two groups. We want to bring out the secure sureness of the first group and the complex situation of the second group.

Here is one question: Do you find any conflict between the Christianity you received and your present situation in real life? Some typical responses of the first group were these:

"No, absolutely not."

"With what I accepted in childhood, yes, but I'm past that stage."
"I might have had at the beginning; but after a few years in Catholic action groups, those small problems disappeared."

"No, or perhaps I should say that sometimes I feel the lack of a more complete formation."

The reader will note that the phrase in the questionnaire, "the Christianity you received," is deliberately ambiguous. Yet it is interpreted as the Christianity received in childhood and it is contrasted with the Christian experience gained in specialized movements of Catholic Action. The sureness of these categorical responses raises suspicions in our mind, especially when we compare them with the responses of those in the second group. Is the lack of conflict due to Christian maturity? Or is it due to their failure to explore the problems more deeply?

Let us look at some of the responses given by the second group of respondents when they were asked the same question:

"Yes, I feel a conflict, not only with what I received in Catholic grammar school *but also with what I accepted later when I was involved in a Catholic Action group.*"

"The Christianity I received gave me a picture of the Church as 'the ark of salvation' which had the solution to every human problem."

"Certainly. The difference between one and the other (i.e., between received Christianity and real-life experience) is the difference between *the static and the dynamic. The evolution that has taken place in the world* recently has *no relation to the survival of a Christianity riddled with a great deal of magic* . . . the latter regarding things that are only taboos as things somehow related to dogmas."

"The Christianity received from the catechism and in parochial schools served for a certain stage, then I left it behind. I admit I still cling to many forms and judgments that are the product of my training in those days. *University life represented my awakening to a new Christianity.* I find it difficult to sum up the elements from that Christianity which are now at a conflict stage today. I would simply make two points: (1) only what I learned in that second stage (university life) sheds light on how the Christian is to live in today's world; (2) what I learned was *neither adequate nor very comprehensive,* but it was enough to prod me and start me looking for an authentic Christian way of life."

Let us consider some of the interesting points in the responses of the second group. Firstly, they do not refer solely to a now resolved conflict between the Christianity received in childhood and their rediscovery of Christianity during their university days. The latter stage, for all its importance, was also a "stage," and it is now being called into question.

Secondly, these responses suggest that further progress in life confronts a person with new situations and new questions which are not adequately handled by the data provided by an earlier stage.

But what exactly are the *deficiencies* of the Christianity lived so far, so that it proves to be inadequate when one confronts new situations? We would readily admit that the responses cited above are not very explicit on this point. But as we proceed to read more of the various responses given, we note a significant fact. Some of the respondents do not define their present situation in terms of a conflict between it and the Christianity of their activist university period. Instead they describe their life today as *infidelity in the present* to the full Christian life they lived in the past. This brings us back by another route to the heart of our problem.

According to the statements of those polled, the "awakening to a new Christianity" in their university days basically meant discovering the person of Christ, the possibility of a personal relationship with him, the necessity of prayer, the communitarian way of life expressed principally in the liturgy, and the whole dimension and import of Christian involvement in the world as well. But one cannot escape the impression that a dualism persists here: between a personal relationship with Christ, prayer, and liturgy on the one hand, and involvement in the world on the other. The Christian life continued to be something lived at the edge of day-to-day life, something lived in a special sphere of existence reserved for the religious element. Then the students moved out into the stage of professional work, marriage, and family life. They now had to confront the real world in all its complexities—difficult decisions, lack of spare time, etc. It now became difficult for them to have recourse to the the vital but quite extra-mundane region in which their Christianity had been situated. The fullness of Christian living which they had experienced in the past was now generating guilt feelings and passing judgment on the impoverishment of their present. What was really happening was that they were confronting a problem which had never really been resolved: How does one encounter God or Christ in the world? What decisive value does the Christian's so-called "profane" activity have for him?.

> "I do not feel any conflict between the Christianity I learned as a Catholic university student, *with all the rediscovery that entailed*, and my life today. I mean, I do not find them contradictory . . . What I do feel, and *what does bother me* today, is a kind of *cooling off* in my personal relationship with Christ. Today I do not share every hour, every task, every joy with him in a felt way as I once used to."

And note the explanation offered by the same respondent:

> "Rarely do I find or *make time* for a tranquil moment of dialogue with the Lord. Rarely do I try to approach him in the Eucharist or the gospel, outside of Sunday. And even then it is difficult for me to establish an interior silence."

Now we might well ask: Isn't a concern for dialoguing with the Lord and meeting him in the Eucharist and the gospel a truly Christian concern? It certainly is. But it is not this *concern* we are analyzing here. What we are analyzing is the respondent's *conception* of dialogue and encounter with God and Christ. And from the context of the statement above it is obvious that this Christian feels he only encounters God in *moments of noninvolvement* with other things. Thus the "cooling off" in his personal relationship with Christ is explained by the fact that he finds it impossible to have such moments.

Let us stress once again that we are not denying the necessity of explicit times for prayer, silence, and separation from daily life. We feel that the reader will agree we approach explicit times of prayer very differently when we take cognizance of our real-life encounter with God in the manifold opportunities to choose for or against others in daily life than when we identify daily life with the profane and see prayer as a time to restore calm to the spirit in a separate realm of the sacred.

Taking this as a presupposition, we can now cite other responses that are rich in content:

"I feel that not everyone has enjoyed the grace that some of us have been given. We were allowed to know the Lord more intimately and to find out what he expects of us . . . For this reason I cannot justify my *present apathy*."

Here again the respondent defines his present situation in exactly the same terms as the one above did. The experience he lived in the past —"the grace that some of us have been given"—is the standard that passes judgment on the present. But a few paragraphs later, this second respondent offers a much more profound evaluation of his crisis:

"Despite that, I think that I and others have been influenced by a whole series of circumstances, for now I see it in part as a *crisis of growth*. Back at the university we lived a life of deep involvement and critical purism, separated from the conditionings that societal life brought home to us later. In the stage of professional work and marriage, a new set of real, concrete options began. We had to leave the *relatively secure framework* we had lived in up to then. Everything was *revolutionized*. We entered a realm in which we saw no general overall solutions, in which *we were forced to search for them*."

This respondent goes on to make statements that embody the same dualism we noted earlier:

"It is not easy to figure out how to live this situation in union with Christ. We once knew how to dialogue with the Lord *through* our temporal and apostolic commitments, and we had our own *readymade 'little way.'* But all this grew much more complicated when we were faced with the many demands of work and our other preoccupations. There was no longer much time for unsullied prayer or for the gospel. When we try to recollect ourselves, we find the Lord a bit strange, and only his will manages to give us a little push now and then."

Now we do not want to deny the real problem of salvaging some time for prayer and reflection in the busy life of the lay person. But we are again forced to ask: Does not the respondent's present conflict come from the fact that his rediscovery of Christianity did not manage to get beyond the dualism of a sacred-profane dichotomy, so that the Christian life continued to be seen as something "above and beyond" the everyday world?

The statements we have just cited are highly significant. Even among Christians who have come a long way in the Christian life—perhaps *especially* among them—we find a conflict between the "religious" conception of Christianity and their real-life experience of a desacralized world. To be sure, their conceptions of the "religious" or the "sacred" do not evince the coarse features we find at other levels. They do not offer a blatantly magical interpretation of Christianity. The "religious" still persists in them to the extent that they have not yet managed to shoulder history, to the extent that they still view transcendence in terms of something *external* to daily life. That is why they describe the conflict between their present life and their university days as one of present *infidelity* to their past life, rather than as an obligation to reformulate the totality of their Christianity on the basis of their present experience.

It is worth noting that this poll, taken just as the liturgical reform was beginning to be implemented at certain levels, bears witness to the twofold effect of this reform that we mentioned in the main section of the Introduction. At first the noticeable increase of participation in the liturgical ceremonies—particularly by young people—erased the suspicion that one was involved in magical rites. But then people began to compare it with the complexity of real-life problems: married life, professional duties, etc. And one could see that the liturgical reform had not managed to overcome the separation between the sacred and the profane. There was no more talk of magical rites, to be sure. But there was talk of separate times and places, so that the conflict was reintroduced in another form.

On the other side of the coin, however, some separation of space and time is required if the sign is to be a sign. We pointed this out in the previous CLARIFICATION. So we are led to reflect on another question. What can fill this space and time in the Christian life with a signification which is justified by its contribution to our secular life?

NOTES

1. The topic of secularization and its import has been treated at length in Volume III of this series (*Our Idea of God*); see especially Chapter II, CLARIFICATION I.

2. See, for example, Edward Schillebeeckx, *Christ the Sacrament of the Encounter with God,* Eng. trans. (New York: Sheed & Ward, 1963) Chapter I; also Michael Schmaus, *Teología Dogmática,* Spanish trans. (Madrid: Rialp, 1961), VI, pp. 28ff. This work is translated as presented in our text, for there does not seem to be a direct English translation of it.

3. Taken in 1966 within the archdiocese of Montevideo, this poll was directed at groups of professional people and university students. It consisted of fifteen questions.

4. See in this volume, Chapter III, CLARIFICATION IV.

CHAPTER ONE

Did Christ Want Sacraments?

No one doubts that Christ's Church has *sacraments*, i.e., sacred rites. The number of them may differ from one Christian confession to another. But if we allow for a possible spread between two and seven in number, it is a fact that all Christians would accept.

Let us examine this fact a bit more closely. An unprejudiced sociologist today would say that the Christian sacraments have obvious parallels in every religion—starting right off with the sacred rites of the Jewish religion in the Old Testament: sacrifices, circumcision, purifications, covenants, drawing lots, etc. He would also say that the parallelism is grounded, at bottom, on the concept of efficacy that these rites entail. Obviously enough we are dealing with *signs* of divine favors that one desires to receive. But these signs have a distinctive feature: under specific circumstances the sign possesses an efficacy that takes it out of the realm of mere knowledge and plants it in the realm of *reality*. In other words, what is signified is also realized, the sign *attracts* grace—even though this realization is invisible in most cases and hence affirmed with the help of faith.

Starting off from this similarity or parallelism, theologians attempt to define the difference or differences that exist between the Christian rites and those of other religions. Needless to say, Catholic theologians are among those engaged in this effort. And perhaps we would not be too far off the mark if we summed up their conclusions by saying that the Christian rites seem to be the only *efficacious* ones. The other rites deceive people; their effect is not truly achieved.

Despite the fact that the word "magic" is used only to designate non-Christian religious rites, one cannot avoid the impression that in the last analysis the difference resides in the fact that Christian "magic" is the only efficacious one.

And it is evident that this efficacy, which does not proceed from the very nature of things (i.e., of the gestures or words used, which only *signify*), can only come from Christ's divine will. But is that the case?

Section I

A complete reading of the New Testament does not suggest, at first glance, that Jesus meant to establish any sacred rites—in the strict sense of the term.

It is not simply a matter of substantiating this point, it is something more. One of the essential principles of the gospel seems to be that the community formed to succeed Jesus is not going to have sacred rites, gestures, or words endowed with divine power. In short, it is not going to have magic signs leading people to salvation.

It is John's Gospel that refers most frequently to baptism and the Eucharist. And there we find Jesus clearly and explicitly formulating the change he is going to introduce into man's relationship with God. When the Samaritan woman (John 4:20 ff.) formulates the problem of the proper place to adore God—Mount Zion or Mount Garizim—she is asking about the efficacy of a rite. For her there is an essential difference in worshipping here as opposed to there, and it cannot be explained in terms of natural causality at all. In one place the rite will achieve its proposed effect; in the other place it will not.

In responding to her, Jesus acknowledges the basis of her question in Palestine's religious past. But he goes on to point out that the time is coming when this question will be superceded by a new type of adoration: i.e., adoration "in spirit and in truth" which is completely liberated from the problem of locality. But in opposing "spirit" to a specific "place," Jesus is obviously opposing much more. Henceforth no ritual specification will be efficacious or ineffective: "God is spirit, and those who worship him must worship in spirit and in truth" (John 4:24). This is the stipulation that counts, as opposed to the physical, local determination which the Samaritan woman wants in order to be sure of the efficacy of her "religious" acts.

What is more, Matthew's Gospel clearly reverses the order of "efficacy" with respect to God: "If, when you are bringing your gift to the altar, you suddenly remember that your brother has a grievance against you, leave your gift where it is before the altar. First go and make your peace with your brother, and only then come back and offer your gift" (Matt. 5:23-24). We minimize the importance of this passage when we envision a brief interlude in the midst of a sacred function.

The fact is that the overall context indicates that man's whole destiny depends on just and cordial relations with his neighbor (Matt. 5:21-23). This is so true that the necessity of righting these relations takes precedence over the strictly religious function.[1] In other words, the natural causality which directs human relationships is more important than the extraordinary causality which governs cultic worship. *Therefore* the latter cannot presume to displace the greater importance of the former by virtue of some "divine" or "supernatural" efficacy. And this holds true in the eyes of God. Hence in the Christian conception it is not possible to scorn the efficacy of authentic human relations for the sake of some loftier efficacy. Any and all sacred magic is completely rejected.

But the New Testament offers us an even clearer and deeper explanation of this in the Epistle to the Hebrews. Like the passage in John's Gospel cited above, this passage is examining the difference between the Old Testament cult and the Christian situation. What unites the two situations is the need man finds for God's help because he is a sinner. The radical difference between them centers around *the repetitiveness or nonrepetitiveness* of the rites designed to obtain this help.

Here is the ancient situation: "For the law contains but a shadow, and no true image, of the good things which were to come; it provides for the same sacrifices year after year, and with these it can never bring the worshippers to perfection for all time. If it could, the sacrifices would surely have ceased to be offered" (Heb. 10:1–2). So "every priest stands performing his service daily. . ." (Heb. 10:12).

While the Christian situation may seem to be the same if we take into account the pastoral handling of the sacraments now in effect, it differs totally from the earlier situation according to the author of this epistle: "But Christ offered for all time one sacrifice for sins, and took his seat at the right hand of God" (Heb. 10:12). Now however illogical it might be, we still could imagine that what Christ obtained remains suspended over our heads as it were, and that we therefore need priests and continuing sacraments to take personal possession of what Christ achieved. But the Epistle to the Hebrews does not see things that way: "For by one offering he has perfected for all time those who are thus consecrated . . . . And where these [sins] have been forgiven, there are offerings for sin no longer" (Heb. 10:14,18). Human beings, then, no longer need sacred intermediaries or sacred mediations.

In other words, if some sort of sacred "magic" did exist at some point, then Jesus Christ was the last and ultimate "magician." He turned us back again to human tasks and human efficacies because he not only *offered* but really *gave* us everything we need from God. Thanks to him, it has penetrated into our inner depths.[2]

Section II

Despite what we have just said, we must accept the fact that the same Church which was expounding these principles as the explicit doctrine of Jesus on the ritual realm was, at the same time, living out religious "signs."

We are deliberately setting up a hypothetical opposition between the terms "rite" and "sign," because we do not know readily whether the religious signs used by Jesus or by the Christian community purported to be rites or something different. But the second alternative does seem to be more in agreement with the doctrine of Jesus picked up by the Church.

What is more, the creation of signs is common to every community. But we cannot tell just from that whether it is meant to convey anything more than a simple intention of expressing something that the community is prepared to recognize. A group may devise some hand signal without intending to institute a rite. Jesus did move around within a certain religious context. But that fact alone is not enough to automatically convert the signs he invented for his community into rites endowed with sacred efficacy, however much obvious significance they may have for that community.

Having made this reservation, we can admit that the Christian community preserved the memory of his typical gestures as well as the memory of his teaching.

First of all, Jesus adopts gestures that are already in use and well known: e.g., the imposition of hands on children and sick people. For that very reason people ask him to do it (Matt. 9:18; 19:13). What is more, the apostles are aware that the risen Jesus has asked them to keep using this gesture (Mark 16:18).

But right here we encounter the first element that is important for understanding the place and significance of the traditional religious gesture in Jesus' public life. If Jesus cures, or liberates people from demoniacal possession, or proclaims the good news, it is all one. It is not a matter of curing for the sake of curing, or even of curing out of pure mercy. When no faith exists, Jesus cannot cure (Mark 6:5). The act of curing is a sign equivalent to proclaiming the gospel message. Hence the response which Jesus gives to the followers of John the Baptist: "Go and tell John what you hear and see: the blind recover their sight, the lame walk, the lepers are made clean, the deaf hear, the dead are raised to life, the poor are hearing the good news " (Mat. 11:45).

That is Jesus' reply to the question: "Are you the one who is to come?" And it is precisely thereby that the traditional imposition of hands acquires its full twofold sense: it relates the act of curing to a plan of God, and to the one who lays on hands as someone sent by God. In this we also see—particularly in Mark's Gospel—that Jesus uses a dialectical rhythm to prevent the act of curing from being turned into a self-contained absolute. He does not want it to stop being a sign, to be turned into a mere effect or efficacy (*cf.* Mark 5:25–34; 6:30–46; 7:31–37, etc). In other words, Jesus wants signs, not rites.

Secondly, this continues to be true—on an even deeper and more unexpected level, if you will—when we are dealing with gestures so specific to the Christian community as baptism and the Eucharist.

The first thing we must do here is divest these words of the "sacred" aura they possess today—insofar as they do not correspond exactly to anything in the profane realm. In the original language of the New Testament (i.e., Greek), we are talking about "bathing" and "giving thanks."

What is more, the Gospel passages which speak most directly of these gestures seem to take pains to frame them in a pedagogical context. They never refer to their sacred effect as if they by themselves could achieve it. In the passage where the risen Jesus orders his disciples to "baptize," for example, he connects the gesture with a preaching duty. "Go forth therefore and make all nations my disciples; baptize men . . . and teach them to observe all that I have commanded you (Matt. 28:19–20; *cf.* Mark 16:15–18).

And there is something else to note. The efficacy at work here in connection with God's plan and man's liberation is attributed *indiscriminately* to the gesture or to faith. So we read in John's Gospel: "In truth, in very truth I tell you, the believer possesses eternal life . . . In truth, in very truth I tell you . . . whoever eats my flesh and drinks my blood possesses eternal life" (John 6:47, 53–54). In this promise of resurrection, for example, the foundation of this promise is attributed to faith in one case and to the gesture in another. To faith in this passage: "No man can come to me unless he is drawn by the Father who sent me; and I will raise him up on the last day . . . Everyone who has listened to the Father and learned from him comes to me" (John (6:44–45). To the gesture in this passage: "Whoever eats my flesh and drinks my blood possesses eternal life, and I will raise him up on the last day" (John 6:54).

The most facile and simplistic interpretation of these passages in current pastoral practice is one which says that here we have two conditions that must be combined. It is as if Jesus, in speaking about faith, had forgotten that eternal life *also* required a gesture: i.e., a rite such as communion. But the obvious interpretation is more complex: Jesus is saying *the same thing* in each case. And if that is the case then communion-as-gesture does not differ from communion-as-faith. It adds nothing in terms of efficacy.

Let us take another example, this one dealing with baptism and its relationship to faith. In the Epistle to the Ephesians we read: "For it is by his grace you are saved, through trusting him . . . Remember then your former condition . . . You were at that time separate from Christ, strangers to the community of Israel . . . Your world was a world without hope and without God. But now in union with Christ Jesus you who were far off have been brought near through the shedding of Christ's blood. For he is himself our peace. Gentiles and Jews, he has made the two one, and in his own body of flesh and blood has broken down the enmity . . . to reconcile the two in a single body to God through the cross" (Eph. 2:8–16).

There is an extraordinary parallel drawn in the Epistle to the Colossians, where the same effect is attributed to baptism. First it notes: "Formerly you were yourselves estranged from God; you were his enemies . . . But now by Christ's death in his body of flesh and blood God has reconciled you to himself " (Col. 1:21–22). Then it adds later: "For in baptism you were buried with him, in baptism also you were raised to life with him . . . And although you were dead because of your sins and because you were morally uncircumcised, he has made you alive with Christ " (Col. 2:11–13).[3]

Once again the simplistic solution would regard the two texts separately. It would add the element of "rite" to the passage from Ephesians and the element of "faith" to the passage from Colossians. But such addition is merely a convenient oversimplification. This is especially evident when we relate it to the two fundamental principles established earlier: (1) the cultic realm has been relativized and put in the service of liberative human relationships; (2) God's saving grace has been conferred in all its plenitude once and for all.

Now if we do not have *two* opposed elements here, then only one solution is open to us. We must say that the primitive Church saw nothing else but faith in its communitarian gestures. Faith in the plain state and faith expressed in gestures were one and the same reality. It was the reality of belonging to the Lord's community, of being liberated by his death and resurrection for the one and only possible acceptance of his person and his message.

A small comparison may help to convey the full import of this point. Teilhard de Chardin offers these accurate and suggestive remarks when he is describing the state of our planet just before man makes his appearance on the scene:

> . . . let us go back to the world as we can imagine it towards the end of the Tertiary period. A great calm seems to be reigning on the surface of the earth at this time. From South Africa to South America, across Europe and Asia, are fertile steppes and dense forests. Then other steppes and

other forests. And amongst this endless verdure are myriads of antelopes and zebras, a variety of proboscidians in herds, deer with every kind of antler, tigers, wolves, foxes and badgers, all similar to those we have today. In short, the landscape is not too dissimilar from that which we are today seeking to preserve in National Parks—on the Zambesi, in the Congo, or in Arizona. Except for a few lingering archaic forms, so familiar is this scene that we have to make an effort to realize that *nowhere* is there so much as a wisp of smoke rising from camp or village.[4]

We find a strange parallel when we look at the first Christian community living in an environment with an imposing array of religious rituals. It has communitarian gestures that signify something and that bear a resemblance to existing forms. But *nowhere* in it do we find a sacred rite in the strict sense of the term. This astonishing little community is claiming that everything has been worked out between God and man once and for all. It does not have "bishops" or "pontiffs," it has "overseers." It does not have "priests," it has "elders." It does not have a "temple," it has family "houses." It does not talk about assembling around the mysterious "real presence" of Jesus; it talks about assembling for "thanksgiving" and "breaking bread."[5]

We might say that it was a community very similar to ours—but with an imperceptible difference that changes everything.[6]

NOTES TO CHAPTER ONE

1. It is worth noting that Jesus attacks the following behavior of the scribes and Pharisees: "Moses said, 'Honour your father and your mother' . . . But you hold that if a man says to his father or mother, 'Anything of mine which might have been used for your benefit is Corban' (meaning, set apart for God), he is no longer permitted to do anything for his father or mother" (Mark 7:10–12).

One might think that Jesus is attacking an arbitrary, misplaced attribution to the religious, but in fact it is something more. Jesus is pointing out that this manner of pretending not to understand historical reality and its possibilities for love, of running away to the sacred instead, is the typical denial of the sacred order that derives from God: "You neglect the commandment of God, in order to maintain the tradition of men" (Mark 7:8). Here he is pointing to a deep-seated tendency in man which is opposed to God and which tries to use the sacred as an evasion from history.

2. *Cf.* Volume II, Appendix III (pp. 201–202).

3. In Acts (2:38) we find a remark of Peter that seems to link the rite of baptism to a sacred efficacy: "Repent and be baptized, every one of you, in the name of Jesus the Messiah for the forgiveness of your sins, and you will receive the gift of the Holy Spirit."

This impression, however, results from one of two possible misunderstandings. In our present-day outlook the first term "repent" signifies only a prior requisite for baptism. In the biblical citation here, as in the other passages cited in this chapter, however, repentance and baptism form one complete sign-reality, and the forgiveness of sins is attributed specifically to this complete sign-reality. We find proof of this in another passage of Acts where Paul is speaking in the name of God: "I send you to open their eyes and turn them from darkness to light . . . so that, by trust in me, they may obtain forgiveness of sins" (Acts 26:18). Baptism is not mentioned here, but that is not because Paul has a different view of its necessity than Peter does (see Acts 16:31–33, in line with the texts cited in this chapter). It is because baptism constitutes the normal expression of the "turning" to the light which brings about the forgiveness of sins.

4. Teilhard de Chardin, *The Phenomenon of Man*, Eng. trans. (New York: Harper & Row, 1959), pp. 152–153.

5. Sacramental theology has not given enough importance to the fact that the early Christian community, which was surrounded and almost overwhelmed by cultures with official cults and mystery religions, moved so far away from the pervasive religious vocabulary and employed a different, wholly secular vocabulary to designate those elements in its life which, at first glance, were the closest to sacred rites and their officiating personnel. Throughout the rest of this book the reader will find repeated use of the word *priest*. But we use it only because we cannot wage a full-scale war against current terminology without making our statement affected and obscure. In principle, and for deep and sound theological reasons, we would have preferred to replace *priest* with some such term as *elder* or *director*, since this term ties in with a profound and decisive experience lived by the early Christian community.

6. "However strange it may seem, the Christian revolution is lay and anti-clerical" (Robert Escarpit, *Ecole laïque, école du peuple*, Paris: Calman-Lévy, 1961, p. 43).

CLARIFICATIONS

I. CHRISTIAN SACRAMENTS AND THE MAGICAL OUTLOOK

According to Catholic theology the seven sacramental signs were identified, explicated, and lived in *one* specific community: the apostolic Church. So when we talk about them in terms of something like the reality of Latin America, can we be sure that we are always talking about *the same thing*?

The problem came up way back in the past, when the masses of the Greco-Roman culture world assimilated this reality. Did they understand the sacramental reality in the same way that the primitive Christian community had? In cultural terms it was a relatively homogeneous cultural world and it was contemporaneous with the Christian community. So when Christianity, with its sacraments and its liturgy, comes to cultures that are quite different and often much more primitive in certain respects, we have a right to be suspicious. We may well ask: When the Christian gestures were transported to cultures where man's whole life was much more sacral and magic-oriented than was life in the Western orbit of Greece and Rome, would not the similarity of the Christian gestures with the rites of other religions have wiped out the religious revolution effected by Jesus?

To take Latin America as an example, we are here talking about sacraments transported over four centures ago to a continent that was as culturally heterogeneous as it could possibly be. If we talk about cultural differences and distances ranging from primitive times to modern times, then dozens of centuries are living together on our continent today. Almost all of these cultural forms have assimilated the "Christian" liturgy in one form or another. That is to say, they took over the liturgy introduced by the conquerors from the Iberian peninsula in the sixteenth century and then went on to amplify and interpret it in a thousand different ways. They have introduced corrections and substitutions, in accordance with the cultural needs and capacities of the immense mosaic that is Latin America.

Now to comprehend, and even more to transform something, one must make distinctions. Well, the fact is that the distinction resorted to most frequently by sociologists and pastors of souls has been a distinction between superstition and Christianity. But alas, this distinction is oversimplistic and irrelevant, even though it does have the advantage of simplifying the priest's task. How does this process of distinction work? It takes the existing heterogeneousness of rites as its starting point and then separates the efficacious ones (the sacraments) from the ineffective and hence erroneous one. Thus hopping around on one foot to obtain a cure is a superstitious act while the anointing of the sick is a sacrament. Wherein lies the difference? In the fact that the first ritual gesture has no efficacy attributed to it while the second does. Superstition means having recourse to ineffective religious rites. It is an error, not in attitude, but in the means employed.

We feel that the root of the difference goes much deeper. It is not simply the mistake of a witch doctor who uses the wrong formula. If a person approaches an "authentic" rite with the same *attitude* that leads other people to a "false" rite, then at bottom he is in the same situation as the latter. He too is obeying a magical impulse. And the opposite holds true too. A person could approach nonsacramental signs with an attitude that is fundamentally the same as the one required in approaching some Christian sacrament.

Hence we must describe the magical situation more in terms of its instinctive and social wellsprings than in terms of the rite it concretely employs. Then we must go on to compare these wellsprings with those that set authentic sacramentality in motion.[1]

There is a constant, reciprocal relationship between two sets of factors here: on the one hand, people's beliefs about an almost permanent interaction between the visible world and invisible "powers" (be they divine or not); on the other hand, the societal organization and the attitudes that compose it.[2]

The mentality of many primitive societies differs from that of "civilized" societies in that its logic is not strictly rational; it does not proceed from cause to effect. Instead it is an affective participation in the world of "invisible powers."

A typical example of this is to be found in the first encounters between natives and the white explorer or hunter. For the indigenous native, the poisoned arrow is not the *cause* of the deer's death, and neither is the bullet of the white man. The white man may be the incarnation of a higher "power," or he may simply be a man aided by a higher "mana"; but in either case his bullets do not *cause* the death of his prey. They are a spell proceeding from the "power" that the adversary possesses.

In such cases how is one to dominate the feeling of insecurity that arises from one's uncontrolled dependence vis-à-vis such powers? Security can return only if one restores one's ties with these beneficent powers through ritual instruments, to which one attributes real power over the mysterious and the divine.

And there is a further factor we must add here. It seems pretty well established[3] that one moment that has a great influence on the child's psychic insecurity is the moment, some time after birth, when it ceases to be shielded by its mother. In so-called "primitive" societies these first critical moments of existence take on a social character and have to do with integration into the community.[4]

In any event this first experience of radical "insecurity" after a child's birth leave its psychic mark on its life. Usually it will seek refuge in the attitudes that are specifically required by its society. Even the sense and import of transcendence can be greater or lesser, depending on the dependence maintained and on the insecurity that the society itself suffers in its attempt to solve its problems by way of causality.

So we get two degrees in the whole matter of ritual procedures, depending on the nature of the "primitivism" in the society where the fundamental phenomenon of insecurity takes place.

The first case is the more primitive one. Here clearly magical procedures are a response to a very rudimentary and mechanistic outlook which seeks to dominate the "powers" through precise gestures, invocations, violent imprecations, and even "sacraments": all these procedures are instruments with a direct effect on the hostile or presumably hostile power. In this situation the belief is wont to be shared by the whole group. It spells out the ritual ceremonies in the minutest detail so that they will be efficacious and so that it may escape its insecurity in and through them. Usually some member of the community is designated to carry them out precisely.

The second case is seen especially when the local society breaks out of its narrow borders and establishes relations with other societies, with urban life in particular. It then purifies and perfects its beliefs, not for the mere whim of purity or perfection but for the sake of displacing its latent insecurity. A certain amount of rationalization transforms its local, particular beliefs and turns them into a universal religion. In this situation rites usually are not given direct, immediate efficacy over the things that threaten man in the visible world. Instead they produce and express an *interior* purification, a state of dependence, which is now demanded by the deity so that he will be beneficent and so that man may escape calamities both in this life and the future life. These calamities are the chastisements that man has merited by his misdeeds.

Undermined internally by the constant threat of many and varied dangers (e.g., the *hubris* or "overweening pride" of the ancient Greeks), man is blocked from attaining complete, thorough felicity. In almost all religions various and distinct rites of purification have developed out of this vivid awareness of man's fundamental frailty. They represent attempts to regain the state of innocence by religious means, for only in that state can there truly and effectively be a favorable relationship with the deity.

Thus while the clearly magical procedures of the first case tie in with a very rudimentary and mechanistic conception of the world,[5] the stylized and intermediate rites of the second case imply greater spirituality. But in both cases rite is still the product of a dualistic conception of the world wherein historical efficacy and a-historical efficacy vie to be the response to man's most basic yearning: security.[6]

In sociological and Christian terms, then, it makes little difference whether man's yearning for security goes in for "superstitions," "private devotions," or "sacraments." The Christian revolution consists in setting in motion, within the community, signs which presuppose that insecurity has been overcome and which commit man to a new risk. It is the risk of bringing a message to the surrounding community. Like the message of the Master himself, it must be a critical message carried to a community where the transcendent has been put in the service of man's security.

II. FIRST AND FOREMOST: A CREATIVE COMMUNITY

Before we encounter sacraments in the gospel, we meet an authentic community which is creating its own distinctive signs under Christ's direction.

Today we use the word "community" when we talk about the Church of Christ. But the sociological reality, deeply linked up with the way in which the sacraments are distributed, does not appear to be a community at all. Restoring the sacraments once again to the finality which Christ gave them means restoring the Church to its character as a community. Put more concretely, it means restoring the Church's character as a congregation of many "base communities" (i.e., grass-roots communities at the local level). For it must be a congregation of real, concrete communities.

In this section we want to describe very briefly and simply the intimate connection between three things: base community, creative reading of the gospel, and its significative re-expression in the liturgy.

The primary trait of a base community is that is constitutes a group. This may not be true at all in the case of people who gather around the Eucharist on Sunday in a large parish; hundreds of people may find themselves next to each other without knowing one another at all. A base community, by contrast, is composed of a restricted number of people who have relationships with each other. *By virtue of this simple fact*, their confrontation with the gospel may differ greatly from the traditional homily approach.

A group, precisely because it is a group, must elaborate what it receives. It must confront, debate, and transform it. A large crowd in a church can simply listen to the Gospel Reading with more or less attention. A group of people must discuss it together, reflect on it, compare it with real life, and see what import a gospel passage has for their own concrete existence as individuals, families, and members of a society.

A large crowd in a parish can listen to the passion narrative on Good Friday and the resurrection narrative on Holy Saturday evening, deriving real benefit in the process. But the attitude of a base community would be different in approaching this narrative. Sooner or later a group of people living in a specific situation, in a concrete place, on a certain date, will necessarily ask itself what these passages are saying to them; what they offer in the way of "good news," "hope," and "faith"; what they point out to them as the requisite new lines of conduct.

This simple fact modifies the educator-pupil relationship, and hence the preaching or proclamation of the gospel. Such a group of people, confronted with a specific passage in the gospel and driven by its own inner dynamism, will elaborate the text that comes to it. Through a more or less lengthy process of search, it will eventually find a new meaning in it. Then the group will be obliged to express the new meaning which it finds in the gospel vis-à-vis its own situation. This is what we were referring to above by "significative re-expression" of the gospel. It means that the group does not mechanically repeat the words of the gospel itself. Instead the group, confronted with this revealed word, translates it into its own situation and context. Thus it continually "re-creates" the gospel, if we may use that expression. The gospel is not a dead letter. It is a word which is incarnated again and again in different situations, different cultures, and different civilizations.

As we see it, this transition from a society of "gospel consumers" to a society of "gospel creators" has deep roots *in the gospel text itself*. The Gospels themselves are four in number. Do we not see here four readings which four Christian communities—at the very least—made out of the Lord's life, death, and resurrection? Does this not show us, at the very start of the Church, the diversity that results when the word of God comes to life in different situations and different contexts?

Perhaps a concrete example from the gospel text itself will help us to understand and appreciate this point. If we read the story about the two men on their way to Emmaus (Luke 24:13 ff.), we find that these two disciples (a base community in miniature) were terribly upset over the big news event of the week—the execution of Jesus, the prophet from Nazareth.

This little community was experiencing the bitter sorrow of a concrete situation, and it found no enlightenment in its faith. The two men put it pointedly: "We had been hoping that he was the man to liberate Israel" (Luke 24:21). Hope had faded away in this little community, which now found itself overwhelmed by a crushing turn of events. The meeting with the stranger would alter this situation. He would explain the Scriptures to them *in relation to the situation they were now living through*. Gradually a new light would dawn. Scripture, which a moment earlier had nothing to say to them, would become a *present, operative, efficacious* word. The stranger certainly did not lead them back over the age-old texts in order to point out their internal import for its own sake. The two disciples, after all, were not interested in a graduate class in exegesis. He reviewed the ancient texts in order to reconstruct the underlying meaning of the group's *present situation*.

The result was that while the passion-happening remained what it had been in material terms, its impact on the lives of the disciples changed completely. They had been hurrying away from Jerusalem; after they got the new interpretation, they went back to Jerusalem. They had been disillusioned; now their hearts were flooded with joy. They had left their fellow-disciples; now they hurried back to them. This base community in miniature will return to its fellow-members and recount the gospel in terms of their own experience. In short, and this is what we are trying to bring out here, they were no longer simply gospel-consumers; now they were gospel-creators too. They would no longer proclaim a stereotyped message to others. Instead they would proclaim the impact of the "good news" on their own lives, and the wholly new orientation it had produced.

This re-expression of the gospel, this "translation" of it in terms of a real-life situation, is characteristic of a base community. What is more, this process within a given situation, culture, and historical moment *must be celebrated*. And here we enter the broad domain of liturgy, which includes the seven sacraments but much more besides. It includes the whole range of what are generally called "liturgical celebrations."

Now what we just said about the gospel is obviously true of its celebration in the liturgy too. The celebration of our new enlightenment and interpretation must be translated into gestures and signs that signify our discovery. So we see that a creative attitude toward faith and the gospel necessarily entails a creative attitude toward liturgical signs. And if we follow through with this logic, then we must admit that it is going to produce an ever-increasing profusion of liturgical signs in the Church. In other words: as the desires and aims of a pastoral effort on the base-community level are realized, in accordance with the vision of the Medellín Conference for example, we will see a flowering of liturgies.

That does not mean we give way to anarchy. In the growing profusion of evangelical interpretations, the magisterium and the hierarchy have an important function to perform. Instead of squelching them, magisterium and hierarchy must harmonize them into a unity that respects diversity within the framework of one faith, one baptism, and one Church. In like manner the magisterium and the hierarchy must continue to create unity out of liturgical diversity; but it must be a dynamic unity rather than a monolithic one. That is the task which faces the Church today.

III. SACRAMENTAL INTOXICATION?

In the perspective of the gospel, the rhythm of sacramental life must be adapted to the external and ultimately decisive function of the Christian *community*.

Looking back at the past which has influenced our situation today, we would have to say that this rhythm was not and still is not respected. We are intoxicated with rites. What is suitable and even necessary in functional, properly balanced proportions becomes toxic when it is administered beyond due limits. From the pastoral standpoint this seems to be the case with respect to the administration of the sacraments.

In the past, and even today in some sectors of the Church, we see a burning desire to "sacramentalize" human beings as quickly as possible. We find this urge in some official circles and among many people. In many instances a child of seven has already received three sacraments: baptism, penance, and the Eucharist. Is it psychically and sociologically possible for these rites to be *sacraments* for the child in most cases—or in any at all? Can these rites be signs of what is happening in the depths of its own life and the lives of other people (even when they do not receive these rites)?[7]

Another feature of this general state of intoxication among Christians has been obligatory frequenting of the Eucharist, quite independent of any perception of its communitarian and historical function. We find this tendency carried to its extremes in Catholic schools where daily attendance at Mass was obligatory. Countless adults, chiefly those who graduated from Catholic schools, have melancholy memories of their forced and passive attendance at the "religious ceremony" called the Mass. And they talk about their regular turnstile visits to the confessional.

We often hear people say: "I have heard enough Masses to last me a lifetime!" And the horrible truth is that their comment is not hyperbole but understatement. They have in fact *heard* many more Masses than are ordinarily compatible with a mature, adult Christian life.

To this we must add another point: the whole *significative* life of the People of God has been centered almost exclusively on the sacraments, on the Mass especially. So true is this that Christian groups and Christian families can think of nothing but celebrating a mass when they wish to commemorate some event. Thus they overlook and neglect a wide-ranging area that has to do with the community's creativity and inventiveness in signifying its faith. For the community must know how to pray in common, and how to fashion a liturgical service that gives expression to its desires, its solidarity, and its participation in the battle between the forces of life and the forces of death.

If what we say is true, then the Church is suffering from sacramental intoxication. With the nature and purpose of the sacraments largely lost (SC 62), what was once functional becomes toxic. And as we contemplate how to restore functionality to them, we should not be alarmed to find a clearcut withdrawal from practice of the sacraments. Such withdrawal allows people to put some distance between themselves and the sacraments; to create room for a real process of search whose positive features we are describing in the pages of this volume.

But this "distancing" imputed to secularization is itself a positive thing insofar as it does not eradicate "sacred" terms but rather gives them a human, historical content. For this is the first step we must take in the linguistic revolution that is necessary if the sacraments are to exercise their signifying function.

In world religions "sacrifice" is the sacred act. People sacrificed a victim to placate the gods and to share in their supernatural potency in some mysterious way. Sacrifice is the religious and ritual act *par excellence*.

Christ annuls this "religious" sacrifice. What he performs is an act of concrete, human love in history.[8] Later, as we have already seen, the term "sacrifice" with its older religious connotations would filter into Christianity once again. Again it would be seen as a sacred act endowed with a peculiar power of its own. Again it would be seen as an act distinct and separate from real life. That is how most people understand the "Eucharistic sacrifice" and the "sacrifice of the Mass." In the meantime the "profane" world, the "lay" world, is showing that it is capable of understanding the new meaning of the word "sacrifice" given by Christ, better than Christians do.

As Claude Tresmontant points out, every human effort requires sacrifice, No matter what field we labor in—art, science, politics, etc.—we may have to sacrifice our family life, our social reputation, or our tranquillity. During his lean years in London, Marx lost two of his children. He *sacrificed* his peace and well-being for a cause he felt to be just. Trotzsky did too. And when Algerian revolutionaries submitted to torture for the sake of a cause they felt to be just, then they were making a sacrifice. In short, "sacrifice" in the Christian sense is not something mystical; it is something concrete, positive, inescapable.

The revolution signified by Christian sacramentality consists in leading the whole community to carry out a prophetic function. And the fact is that the prophetic function entails sacrifice, in its secular sense. If a prophet espouses the cause of justice in a tribal or national community that is collectively unjust, then he knows he is running a risk. This was true in the time of Jeremiah. It is still true today for the political figure who fights against some crime or injustice.

Every effort on behalf of justice and truth inevitably evokes resistance from those who have their own interests to preserve, who do not want people to call into question the conceptual system or the unjust order to which they have become habituated. When Jesus of Nazareth was led to the place of execution, he verified this fundamental law that is operative in the human world such as it is. He was aware of this law and did not dodge it. To bring his work to completion, he chose to accept the law that rules in man's world: every positive effort on behalf of justice and truth encounters violent resistance. And the more profound and decisive the required work of transformation is, the more violent the resistance will be. Understood in this sense, sacrifice ceases to be something occult or magical. It becomes the act of a human being who is fully exercising his liberty.

It is an historical fact, and a policy bequeathed to us from the life of the apostolic Church, that the pastoral ministry of the sacraments generally follows the pastoral ministry of the word. So to rescue such words as "sacrifice," "consecration," "salvation," and "evil" from the sphere of the sacred would, paradoxically enough, enable us to re-establish a bridge between man's fundamental situations (now designated by words that were formerly sacred) and a language associated for centuries with the sacramental liturgy.

If one will not accept this task, if one seeks primarily and at all costs to erect a sacred, sacramental language, then he is contributing to the intoxication of which we have been speaking. Its essential hallmark is that it does not respect a rhythm which begins with the word that wells up from man's real-life experience.[9]

IV. SACRAMENTS FOR THE COMMUNITY

It would seem to be an incontestable fact, both pastorally and sociologically, that the sacraments have taken over a place and preeminence in Christian life that does not really belong to them. It would also seem that our present-day pastoral reform is posing the problem in these terms: What is the proper dosage of community and sacramentality in a well-balanced formula?

Proof of the latter assertion can be seen in the fact that we are still trying to establish a pastoral ministry to "popular religiosity" alongside a pastoral ministry to "base communities." It is also proven by the fact that proposed pastoral plans, with only rare exceptions, start out from the reality of the parish and then spread to complementary areas—without ever questioning whether this parochial reality exists. And the fact is that the pastoral ministry which constitutes the basis of the parish has for centuries been what we now call a "popular" pastoral ministry, one based on the territorial distribution of the sacraments and their administration.

A final proof is furnished by the fact that some bishops, backing away from the outlook of the Medellín Conference,[10] have presented the focus on base communities in a different light. They do not present it primarily as a basic, intrinsic dimension of Christ's Church. Instead they present it as the remedy needed *today* to combat the herd approach introduced by the requirements of a consumer society and, in particular, by the media of social communication. Thus they can freely allocate for this remedy a certain share of the resources of personnel, time, energies, and money that the Church has as it now is.

Here, as in many other points of theology (mainly postconciliar theology), the problem of giving both "this" and "that" its due obscures the formulation of the radical problem: What do we do to make sure that the existing setup has meaning or regains its meaning? In terms of the latter approach, dosage is the least important thing. The important and decisive thing is how to arrive at something meaningful and significative.

The gospel, as we have seen it in this chapter, does not show us two elements that must be combined. It shows us a real community to which Jesus offers *all* his energy in generous measure. And it shows us sacramental signs that are comprehended *solely* as a function of this real community and to the extent that it is a real community.

Hence the pastoral problem of the sacraments, insofar as it is formulated in the way we have just criticized, does not really have any solution. Having reached this point, we can proffer a seemingly paradoxical statement: strictly speaking, we do not feel that there is a crisis *with respect to the sacraments* at all. There is indeed a crisis, a crisis that may be even deeper and more serious. For our difficulty and our crisis with respect to the sacraments does not stem from the sacraments or their decrepit liturgical entourage. It stems from the fact that we do not see the necessary correspondence between what they signify and the reality of the Christian community in the world.

At our parish Masses we worship the God who "unites us in love," when the fact is that we are nowhere close to such unity or love at all. The Eucharist seems to be totally devoid of meaning, not because it is a sacrament but because it does not flow out into any real community.

We talk about "common union"; but for all our liturgical changes it is precisely this "common union" that is missing. We talk about "community Mass," as if it were not a redundant phrase. And what is even more important, we do not see this community which, if missing, precludes any meaningful use of the very word "Mass."

It was this crisis that led Camilo Torres to ask to be relieved of his priestly functions. Strictly speaking, it was not a sacramental crisis but a far deeper one. It is the crisis we ourselves face. Camilo Torres never ceased to find the sacraments themselves meaningful. What he found meaningless was the notion of continuing to dole out sacraments to Christians who were evidently closed to love, insensitive to injustice, and unfeeling toward the poverty and anguish of their dispossessed fellows.

In short, what is plaguing us is not a crisis over the sacraments but a crisis over the *coherence and meaningfulness of the Christian community*. There are times when it seems that our yearning and zeal for ritual reform and liturgical renewal is a superficial way of solving a much deeper problem. For it enables us to hide from the real problem: the problem of community. Cultic reforms and the thrust toward a simpler, purer ritual are good and even necessary. But we will not progress very far with them. The process of liturgical reform seems to be nearing the end of its course. And at its end we may see even more clearly that we have not achieved the most important thing of all—even in terms of sacramental life itself. Liturgical reform will not resolve the crisis. Its real and undeniable usefulness may in fact be to heighten it. For with each passing day the absence of authentic Christian community will become even clearer. Only the intrinsic and functional coherence of the latter will enable us to rediscover and live the mystery embodied in the sacramental signs.

For this reason we feel it would be worthwhile to stop here for a moment and try to define or describe this community, which we have advanced as the presupposition for, and the fruit of, the sacraments.

Let us agree that of late we have abused the term *community*. We do so when, for example, we apply it to something so formless as the so-called "parish community"—thereby referring to a crowd of people who attend Sunday Mass together without really knowing each other before or after. We use the same exaggerated latitude when we hasten to apply the term *community* to any group of Christians who get together for reflection or study.

Without denying that the latter kind of group can be the first step toward community, we feel that Christian community is something much more. Its definition springs from the gospel statement: "If there is love among you, then all will know that you are my disciples" (John 13:35).

Two words would seem to be an indispensable part of any Christian community. One is *sharing*, the other is *giving*. And both must be taken in a very concrete sense, not in any mythical or symbolic sense. In other words, the Christian community is characterized by two things. Firstly, it must be a community of *mutual aid* in which people practice the dimensions of real encounter and fraternal love, not simply by reading or reflecting, but by proferring real, concrete help. This may even go so far as to entail sharing their goods in common. (This would not have to take a juridical form, even as it did not in the primitive Church, and it would not be restricted to money.)

Secondly, such a community cannot exist for its own self-satisfaction. It must carry out a mission. The mutual aid of the community is not its own intrinsic justification; it is not confined to the ambit of the faith community. Thanks to it, the community ought to be able to free itself on every level (material, moral, etc.) so that it can exercise service to the rest of mankind.[11] If a community did not have this goal that transcends itself, it would rapidly run down. In any case, it would not be a Christian community.

But are we not making too radical a proposal when we posit real, visible, concrete community life as a basic exigency of Christian life rather than as the ideal of perfection and holiness? Are we not asking too much?

Considering the fact that we human beings have our limitations, that we are a mixed bag of love and egotism, of spirit and flesh, we would all readily admit that we will never be able to achieve perfect

Christian community. Every time we move up a step, Christ will come
to us again for a talk. Enlightened anew by the Spirit, we will see another
step ahead of us, and then another, and then still another. God save
us from the false belief that we have achieved the perfect Christian
community!

One of the constants in Christian existence is the fact that we live
a permanent process of tension and striving, a continuing struggle with
its own inner dynamism. Christian existence can never measure itself
against the bare minimum required to justify the label "Christian." It
must measure itself against the maximum reality, as yet unattained:
Christ, the image of the Father's perfection.

But precisely because our point of reference is this maximum rather
than the upper limits of our own efforts or the efforts of mankind,
we must also agree on something else. Considering the reality of our
Christianity today, we must admit that there is a threshold still to be
crossed, a risky change to be worked out, a communitarian conversion
to be accomplished. In other words, we must admit that we Christians,
with all our weaknesses, are being summoned to work up and live out
this community of sharing and giving.

Now it is our belief that such a Christian community will not suffer
any sacramental crisis or have any major difficulties about the meaning
of the sacraments. It will see the meaning quite clearly. Our present-day
problem will have evaporated into thin air.

It will undoubtedly be such communities that will know how to find
the best and most significant forms of sacramental expression. But in
all probability they will not be overly concerned about external transformation. They will not feel the desperate urge to renovate and purify
the liturgy that drives many Christians today.

Past experience proves that a true community was able to find expression even in the old liturgy. Even the most traditional and baroque
Mass can be charged with life and meaning when it is being celebrated
by a true community of brothers. There is little need for rapprochement
and explanation when it is an assembly of brothers and sisters who
are working together, playing together, struggling together for the same
life-ideal, and shouldering together the burdens of Christian sacrifice.

NOTES

1. This we must do before we face up to a key pastoral problem: i.e., deciding whether the shift from one attitude to the other is possible by a mere process
of transition, or whether it implies a radical break that pastoral practice must accept and pave the way for. See Chapter IV, CLARIFICATION III.

2. Ethnology gave order and structure to the global study of primitive social
organizations and to the wellsprings of spontaneous attitudes. This expanded the
panorama provided by studies devoted to specific regions, integrating them into an
overall view of man's societal life.

3. Here social psychology combines with ethnology to describe the origin of
certain attitudes and motivations that are extremely powerful and widespread.

4. Different ways of weaning babies (ranging from gradual to very abrupt)

and of swaddling them (ranging from tight binding to complete freedom and looseness) were considered data that characterized the society type. A rigid, authoritarian society on the one hand, and a less vertically structured society on the other, would handle these key moments and aspects of childhood differently. They would integrate the child into the community in different ways. Insecurity is overcome or not, depending on how these processes work out.

    5. In Latin American society Christianity acquired full citizenship rights. But often it did so in a formal, juridical way. Countless attitudes tied up with beliefs proper to ancient or even primitive societies crop up again and again—not only in rural areas but also in urban centers. Consider Uruguay, for example. The majority of its population is made up of immigrants from Europe who arrived here relatively recently. Yet the proliferation and popularity of private devotions to the saints clearly manifests the latent power of magic, which is rooted in man's quest to overcome adversity by some pathway other than technical expertise. One saint is the patron saint of good luck, another is one's protectress in storms. Ancient prayers of the Church and special blessings help to cure indigestion and other embarrassing discomforts. Other persons besides priests, adept at making the sign of the cross and reciting the proper Latin formulas in secret ceremonies, can protect the interested customer from evil spirits. In the local community they can acquire great status. In times of trouble and affliction people will run to them for help with greater or lesser regularity, depending on the general cultural level of the locale. In some areas the medical doctor may take a back seat to the "healer," whose high reputation is based on his ability to divine things and to exercise dominion over the unknown and the transcendent.

    6. The fatalistic conception of man and the universe can also exert influence on religions of a universal cast, and even on highly secularized civilizations. The individual feels that his destiny is marked out for him, and that no human effort can change it. It is beyond his reach and his capacities. His longing for a more favorable destiny will depend wholly on an inner relationship with the deity or fate, and on a respect for laws that are completely different from those that regulate technical skill and know-how: e.g., the laws of astrology and the dictates of one's horoscope.

    7. For this reason there seems to be much positive good in the pastoral approach that spreads out reception of the sacraments of initiation more realistically, following the child's rhythm of growth in the process of incorporating him into the ecclesial community. Baptism, confirmation, and Holy Eucharist should mark stages of increasing participation and respect the gradual rhythm of human life. The opposite outlook can only be grounded on a semimagical conception of the sacraments.

    The first outlook is becoming more and more widespread. But we wonder if it has been thought through to its ultimate conclusions. For example: What would happen in our children and in the Christian community if the former, instead of being obliged to attend Mass, were prevented from participating until they reached the level of Christian maturity that corresponds to the last sacrament of initiation—i.e., the Eucharist?

    8. "He had always loved his own who were in the world, and now he was to show the full extent of his love" (John 13:1).

    9. See ahead, Chapter IV, CLARIFICATION I.

    10. *Cf.* Medellín's document on Joint Pastoral Planning, MED II, 221–233.

    11. A specific service, on which see Volume I, Chapter III.

CHAPTER TWO

Efficacious for What?

The Christian who approaches the sacraments today ordinarily has the feeling that he is doing something useful and even necessary for eternal life. So far as we know, the Christian living in the primitive Church saw these distinctive signs of his community in a different light. He did not see them as something useful or necessary; rather, he saw them as spontaneous gestures in a community that was in possession of eternal life.[1]

The difference may seem to be minimal, but in fact it is not. Whether we consider it in terms of our crisis today, or in terms of the panoramic history that runs from those early Christian signs to our sacraments of today, the difference is quite significant. A brief look at this history can and should shed light on our present crisis.

Section I

In the previous chapter we arrived at a negative conclusion: the distinctive signs of the Christian community were not experienced or lived as sacred rites. But these signs did exist and they were important nevertheless. This is proven by the countless direct and indirect allusions of the New Testament to the significative and uniform gestures of the Christian community.

So we may ask: What was their practical and significative content? And in answering this question we shall limit our investigation to the three signs whose practice and signification appear to be most fully developed in the New Testament. The first two were represented by significative gestures that took place within the community: Baptism (really "bath"), and Eucharist (really "thanksgiving," "participation," "breaking of bread"). The third seems to have taken place outside the community: marriage. But when it was introduced into the community and lived there, then it acquired a new communitarian sense and a new communitarian function.

1. If one understands the normal social function of signs and gestures, he will not be surprised to find that the three signs under study
here had the function of integrating the individual into the Christian
community. In other words: participation in them and creation of the
community itself were synonymous. Interest in the sacraments was
nothing else but interest in the matter of belonging to the community.

This is evident in such texts as the following. Paul writes this to
the Corinthians about baptism: "For indeed we were all brought into
one body by baptism, in the one Spirit, whether we are Jews or Greeks,
whether slaves or free men. . . . Now you are Christ's body" (1 Cor.
12:13,27). And to the Galatians he writes: "Baptized into union with
him . . . you are all one person in Christ Jesus" (Gal. 3:27–28).

To relate communion—*common union*—with the constitution of the
Christian community, the new covenant people, is a classic procedure.
In one case Paul says: "When we bless 'the cup of blessing,' is it not
a means of sharing in the blood of Christ? When we break the bread,
is it not a means of sharing in the body of Christ? Because there is
one loaf, we, many as we are, are one body; for it is one loaf of which
we all partake" (1 Cor. 10:25). Later he adds, quoting Jesus: "This cup
is the new covenant sealed in my blood" (1 Cor. 11:25).

Marriage too shows up as a multiplying refraction of the original
body that Christ forms with his community: "Men also are bound to
love their wives, as they love their own bodies . . . that is how Christ
treats the church, because it is his body, of which we are living
parts . . . and the two shall become one flesh.[2] It is a great truth that is
hidden here. I for my part refer it to Christ and to the church, but
it applies also individually. Each of you must love his wife as his very
self " (Eph. 5:28–33).

2. If the function of the principal communitarian gestures is one
and the same, our immediate assumption would be that the signification
of each one should differ. But that is not the case. Despite the diversity
of the gestures, the nucleus to which they allude remains invariable.
It is the death and resurrection of Christ reproduced in our own lives.

Here is the meaning of baptism as Paul describes it to the Colossians:
"In baptism you were buried with him, in baptism also you were raised
to life with him through your faith in the active power of God who
raised him from the dead" (Col. 2:12). And in another epistle he writes:
"By baptism we were buried with him, and lay dead, in order that,
as Christ was raised from the dead . . . so also we might set our feet
upon the new path of life" (Rom. 6:4).

The breaking of bread has the same import and signification: "This
is my body, which is for you. . . . Every time you eat this bread . . . you

proclaim the death of the Lord, until he comes" (1 Cor. 11:24–26).

And it is the same with matrimony, where the meaning refers explicitly back to that of baptism: "For the man is the head of the woman,
just as Christ also is the head of the church. . . . Husbands, love your
wives, as Christ also loved the church and gave himself up for it, to consecrate it, cleansing it by water and word, so that he might present the
church to himself all glorious" (Eph. 5:23–27).

What does all this mean? Undoubtedly the most likely hypothesis
is that these gestures represent initiation into ever deeper and more
complete degrees of comprehending and expressing in one's life the
central message of faith. And that central message is that Christ laid
down his life and the Father raised him up again from the dead.

3. Thus we can see the twofold aspect of the gesture. It fashions
the community and has no other efficaciousness outside of membership
in the community. It signifies what is the basis of the community: i.e.,
the faith that the Jesus-happening is the very structure of man's existence.

Stationed at the doorway of the community, as it were, the gestures
explain why the primitive community in operation saw itself differently
than we do today. If we were to describe the Christian community in
operation today, we would talk about *liturgy*, that is, about sacraments.
Paul, on the other hand, does not. He does not ignore the fact that
the Lord's meal has its place in the assembly of the faithful. But he
presents this assembly moving on from the memory of Christ to the
exercise of the charisms and talents which God provides so that the community may carry out its function. And the fact is that there is no mention
of the sacramental realm in the theoretical enumeration of these charisms
or in the concrete description of a community operating as an assembly.

This is what Paul has to say to the Corinthians about the charisms:
"One man, through the Spirit, has the gift of wise speech, while another,
by the power of the same Spirit, can put the deepest knowledge into
words. Another, by the same Spirit, is granted faith; another, by the
one Spirit, gifts of healing, and another miraculous powers; another
has the gift of prophecy, and another ability to distinguish true spirits
from false; yet another has the gift of ecstatic utterance of different
kinds, and another the ability to interpret it. But all these gifts are
the work of one and the same Spirit" (1 Cor. 12:8–11).[3]

The Church *goes to work* with what God gives. Her activity is not
sacramental, even though it is the sacramental that fashions her into
a community united around the paschal mystery. What the Church does,
her labors, are not sacraments; rather, it is the sacraments that fashion
human beings into a Church.

Thus the concrete description of a Christian community at work
in its assembly does not dovetail at all practically with a present-day

description. Paul begins by saying that the fundamental, universal, supreme capacity which should be operative in the community is love (1 Cor. 12:31 and 13:13). But there also exists a hierarchy of capabilities for the concrete implementation of love in the Christian community. The most important and universal of these capabilities is that of the *prophet* (1 Cor. 14:1,5). He is the one who is able to look into events, to discern their deeper, underlying meaning, and to relate them to God's plan.[4]

Hence the relations between a nonbeliever and the Christian community are to a certain extent, as far as Paul sees it, directly opposed to those existing today. For today the community gathers together almost exclusively in terms of the sacramental realm. But Paul says: "So if the whole congregation is assembled and all are using the 'strange tongues' of ecstasy, and some uninstructed persons or unbelievers should enter, will they not think you are mad? But if all are uttering prophecies, the visitor . . . hears from everyone something that searches his conscience and brings conviction, and the secrets of his heart are laid bare. So he will fall down and worship God, crying. 'God is certainly among you!' " (1 Cor. 14:23–25).

This is the precise, carefully balanced image that comes out of the New Testament writings. It pictures a community that goes about its work out of love, interpreting history on the basis of a common code-key and an internal cohesiveness that is achieved and expressed in the sacraments.

Section II

In the subsequent history of the Church during the first few centuries, we can see that the sacraments imbue everything with their *signification*. Despite the problems and deviations that crop up, they, like faith and along with it, are a real key to what membership in the Christian community represents. They differ from one another primarily as distinct levels of initiation into the *same* essential nucleus that goes to make up the Church—and not as instruments for particular graces.

Conscious knowledge of the paschal mystery and the concomitant responsibilities were not the same at every level of initiation. In baptism one moved from the situation of the catechumen to the status of a faithful member. Then one received the Holy Spirit and a concomitant set of specific ecclesial tasks (Acts 6:3–6; 8:14–17; 10:44–48; 13:2–3; and *passim*). At the level of communion a total integration was realized and reiterated; now one had the responsibility of bearing the badge of "brother" before the world. But this full integration was not a definitive

thing, not a security blanket. One ran the risk of being separated from
the community if his "representation" did not accord with the message
that the Christian community wanted to transmit (1 Cor. 5). So there
was re-initiation at the level of penance, which had its own function,
import, and responsibilities. One of them was the firm purpose of changing one's way of life, which was authenticated by the difficulty of a
second or even third reintegration.

Thus the preparation of the Christian—i.e., catechesis—was carried
out by degrees in accordance with the signs that marked the start of
each new stage.[5]

As time went on, however, interpretation of the "sacramental" realm
developed and expanded. First of all, we should not underestimate the
impact of all the surrounding religiosity, which was unanimous in interpreting the signs of the Christian community as efficacious religious
rites. Right at the beginning of the Church Paul himself had to fight
against the notion that baptism had an almost automatic religious effectiveness (cf. 1 Cor. 1:11–17; 47).[6]

Secondly, during this period the Church shifted from being a small
community to becoming a mass religion. Grace, given totally once and
for all, was supposed to liberate man from the divisive burden of having
to resort incessantly to the sacred in order to obtain divine aid. It launched
man toward a new creativity, which was now made possible in two ways:
(1) by virtue of the intrinsic liberative quality of grace;[7] (2) by virtue
of the fact that man was no longer monopolized by the "religious" task
of procuring divine life. But mass religiosity on the popular level did
not appreciate this creativity, this open ground, this insecure responsibility. Not unsurprisingly the herd mentality went back to the idea
of a privileged way to obtain help and salvation from God. For it the
Church was no longer the locale where God's message creates new dimensions and new responsibilities vis-à-vis history. Rather, it was the locale
where faith and rites, practiced with precision, are in themselves directly
valid for obtaining God's favor.[8]

The Church paid a price here for its new universality. It permitted
these two different conceptions and uses of the sacraments to exist alongside each other. This accounts for the ambiguity surrounding a controversy which raged in the third and fourth centuries. It was to leave
its mark on later theology and subsequent sacramental practice. The
question at issue was this: When Christians baptized by heretical ministers
were converted to orthodox Christianity, did they have to be baptized
again?

Interestingly enough it was Saint Cyprian, the bishop of Carthage,
who was the principal advocate of repeating the sacramental sign of

baptism. What is even more interesting, it was during this controversy that he, in defense of his thesis (which was later to be rejected by the Church), coined the famous dictum: "No salvation outside the Church." The point of the dictum was that since no one can give what he does not have, it was illogical to think that someone excluded from the Church could communicate to others a saving grace which Christ had associated with the authentic community that carried on his work.

A rebuttal was elaborated by Augustinian theology, and it was to win out in this controversy. At bottom it followed the lead of the Epistle to the Hebrews, to which we have already referred. It said that the notion of "priest" in the strict sense of the word—i.e., of an obligatory intermediary between human beings and God—is not a Christian notion. For grace to reach man in reality, all that is needed is the work of Christ (already carried out) and man's acceptance of it (through his good will). Thus no one will lack grace through the fault of a third party.

Here patristic theology dissociated salvific efficacity from the good or bad dispositions of the minister[9] entrusted with the sacramental sign, and it put the stress on the aspect of sacramental *validity*. It seemed to accentuate the sacred efficacy of a sacrament and its detachment from any and all human efficacy. When the rite was performed, grace was received: that seemed to be the simplest explanation of the decision reached.

Section III

The whole context was certainly ambiguous. Or, if you prefer, it was composed of two different levels. And it was within this context that theology and sacramental practice would develop through the Middle Ages. The problem would be posed once again by the Reformation controversy, and this would lead to the definitions of Trent.

Initiation into the mystery of Christ's community, reception of different" graces that were necessary for life: Were they really two opposed things? Up to a point they were at least different. And the life of an established Church, accompanying the Christian life of each succeeding human generation, pointed toward the second feature.

Leaving aside popular deviations and admitting that every grace is paschal (effecting in us the reality lived by Christ in his death and resurrection), we still must admit it would be improper to say that a baptized infant already possesses the "paschal" grace of matrimony. The grace which the infant possesses *concretely* is the grace symbolized by its passage through water—water being the sign *par excellence* of a new life in the eyes of the ancients. In other words: the grace possessed in the concrete took the form of the sign that manifested it.

Now even though every grace is already given in the paschal happening of Christ, patristic theology did not maintain that the intimate connection between sign and concrete grace amounted to an automatic synchronism.[10] It is possible—and it is almost always the case—that the grace of God is already there when a person receives the sacramental sign. Nevertheless the grace is not complete on the level of the ecclesial community so long as it is not united with its sign, so long as it is not lived out in its signification.

Thus we can and should say that *grace in the concrete*, the grace that man needs for his present state in life—entering the Church, assuming full communitarian responsibility, marrying, etc.—achieves its effective concretization with the sign. Thus the sacraments, signifying grace, confer it.[11] In reality it is Christ who confers it, but its concretization in terms of the community depends on the sign and comes with it.

When the Church came to be identified with the occidental world for all practical purposes, however, its essential external function pretty much disappeared from view. The Church saw herself as the depository of grace, and the masses that belonged to her thought that the function of the sacraments, received with all the conditions required for validity, was to give them possession of this privileged grace.

It was in this ambiguous framework that church practice, in the eleventh century, came to fix the seven sacramental signs which it judged to have derived from the Lord's own will in some way or another.[12] Practice has remained fixed right up to our own day; interpretation would continually fluctuate between the religious revolution introduced by Christ and the spontaneous attitudes of popular religiosity.[13]

Section IV

The debate over the sacraments at the time of the Reformation attempted to dispel this ambiguity. From the Catholic side, Trent put an end to debate by defining three central points: (1) all the sacraments were instituted by Christ (Denz. 844); (2) the sacraments are seven, no more and no less (Denz. 844); (3) faith in the divine promise is not enough to obtain grace, but the sacraments confer it *ex opere operato*, that is, by the very performance of them (Denz. 851).

Taken as they read, and on the condition that one does not make them say anything except what they do say strictly and really, these three enunciations are consistent with the understanding of the sacramental realm that we found in the primitive Christian Church and even in the New Testament. This is true even though they put the emphasis on points that stem primarily from the debate with Protestants, and thus have a certain "negative" tone.

This "negative" concern, which is classic in theology and which is necessary for any further development, is particularly important here. For the fact is that people fill in the "gaps" in these enunciations with deductions that do not belong to Trent, thus managing to make theory dovetail with existing sacramental practice. In other words, they manage to justify what is already being done in practice.

Here is one example. People say: "The sacraments are seven because Christ instituted seven—no more and no less." In reality the Tridentine statement affirms that behind all the existing sacraments—that is, seven—there is an intention of Christ who institutes them. It does not define that he instituted them one by one until he got to seven.[14] Latent in the aforementioned "deduction" is the desire to justify a practice in which the Church has value by virtue of the sacraments it provides, rather than the sacraments having value by virtue of the community that they create and set in operation. The notion that Christ instituted the sacraments one by one in isolation, for their own sake, is an unconscious attempt to establish a direct relationship between savior and rites without having to go through the Church.

Here is a second example. People say: "The sacraments are seven because only these seven signs confer grace *ex opere operato*; every other sign of grace is efficacious only *ex opere operantis*, that is, by virtue of the psychological change which the sign produces in the person who receives it." Here again a bridge has been illegitimately placed between two affirmations; they have been connected with a "because" that does not belong there. "The sacraments are seven." "The sacraments are efficacious *ex opere operato*."

The aim here is to completely differentiate the sacraments, *in terms of salvific efficacy*, from any and every other mode of signifying grace. It is as if the other signs of grace run up against a wall. No matter how much good will is placed in them, they are not capable of "attracting" the grace that man needs but which God has restricted to *determined signs*. The use of the illegitimate "because" and the subsequent differentiation of the sacraments from all other signs enable people to justify a magical conception of the sacramental realm. This magical conception, which is not described as being such, is the one that corresponds to a major portion of our present pastoral approach.

Here is a third example, which may well be the most critical and decisive one in this whole realm. People say: "In the sacraments grace is conferred *ex opera operato*; that is, by the act performed by the minister of the sacrament; that is, in most cases, by the act performed by the priest." The oversimplification here is effected by separating the principal phrase from the twofold context in which it was framed by Trent. First of all, the *ex opere operato* of the conciliar statement is explained and limited by a "but," which sets it up in opposition to the affirmation (attributed to Protestants) that faith without the sacraments is sufficient for grace. Secondly, the previous canon refers to the fact that grace is "always" given in the sacraments to "all"; and it attributes this to the fact that grace has no obstacle or condition from God's side. In other words, it is given—by virtue of the work performed *by Christ*.

Taking into account this twofold context, and presupposing that grace is given on the one hand and that a person has good will in his faith on the other, we can then ask: How could it possibly happen that without the sacraments such a person would not obtain the grace he needed? The simplistic response would be that it can be due to the absence of a minister with the divine powers to transmit it.

But if we frame the affirmation about the *ex opere operato* efficacy of the sacraments within the context of the Council of Trent, and even more within the context of Scripture and church tradition, it refers primarily to the constitution of the Church. We have already had occasion to examine the theological connotations of the obligation to be a member of the Church, in terms of salvation. We saw that it was not to be interpreted as submission to some restrictive condition imposed by God, which in turn conferred a privilege on the members. Rather, it was to be interpreted as a responsibility incumbent on us if we wanted our love to be efficacious.[15]

In other words, one cannot possess the faith and reject the Church because authentic faith presents the Church as a particular and specific service to the rest of mankind. Thus the fact that God wills to give grace through the sacraments means nothing else but that he intends to give his grace as the grace "of the Church": i.e., as grace which fashions a Church in the service of the rest of the human community.

Hence Vatican II did not have to deny or negate Trent in order to re-establish the authentic use of the sacraments. It does acknowledge a problem: "With the passage of time . . . there have crept into the rites of the sacraments . . . certain features which have rendered their nature and purpose less clear" (SC 62). What is "less clear" is not their efficacy in terms of grace[16] but their "pedagogical purpose." Without the latter being understood, the grace that comes in the sacrament would simply be God's response to man's good will. It would not be "Christian" grace, which is a conscious introduction to ecclesial life and to its function centered around the paschal mystery.

The only thing is that this renewal is not and cannot be the result of any "liturgical reform." It must come from the transformation of the entire Christian community.

NOTES TO CHAPTER TWO

1. *Cf.* Volume II, Chapter II and Chapter III, CLARIFICATION II. "This letter is to assure you that you have eternal life" (1 John 5:14).

2 Here as elsewhere in Scripture, the term "flesh" refers to an affective participation and sharing. It does not refer directly to sexual intercourse. See Volume II, Chapter II, CLARIFICATION I.

3. In a briefer formula: "apostles . . . prophets . . . teachers . . . miracle-workers . . . those who have gifts of healing, or ability to help others or power to guide them, or the gift of ecstatic utterance of various kinds" (1 Cor. 12:28).

4. On this knowledge of God's plan for history see Volume II, Chapter II. Section II of the main article: also Chapter III, CLARIFICATION III.

4. The catechesis for these various stages was called "mystagogical catechesis." The most famous set of them was attributed to Saint Cyril of Jerusalem, even though one or more may really come from one of his immediate successors.

6. See Volume I, Chapter III, CLARIFICATION IV.

7. See Volume II, Chapter I, Section III of the main article.

8. Augustine mentions, and the Church was later to reprove, the abusive practice of delaying baptism until the hour of death. The underlying idea was to receive its "effect" at the most decisive moment of one's life. This practice is a clear indication that man's age-old "religious" tendency toward mass-oriented practices had made inroads among Christians.

9. Later, around the beginning of the thirteenth century, there would be a seemingly more precise formulation of what was required of the minister of the sacraments. He must *do what the Church does*. This formulation was later sanctioned by Trent (Denz. 854).

Much ink has been spilled trying to delimit the exact dividing line between nonsacrament and sacrament in this sense. In general, inquiry and discussion have centered on the subjective aspect of intention. However, if we take account of the existence and value of the sacraments of desire as well as the comman theological principle that God does not deny his grace to those who show good will on their part, then the decisive feature of the minister's action cannot depend on his secret, subjective intention; it must lie in what he obejctively performs. Doing what the Church does means placing the sacrament in its significative context, in its ecclesial functionality. This point seems to be ignored in the oft-debated case of the apostate priest who "consecrates" wine in a bar or bread in a bakery. For this argument assumes that his *subjective* intention of consecrating is enough. But that is not *doing what the Church does* with consecrated bread and wine.

10. And so, for example, the Church recognizes the "reviviscence" of the sacraments. The sign can be received in the context of the ecclesial community, but without an authentic interior disposition. When the latter disposition does finally show up, the external sign does not have to be repeated; it is completed by the interior disposition and by the grace that then reaches man. Again we have what constitutes a sacrament: signified grace. And the reverse happens too, as the reader will see from what follows.

11. Saint Thomas's formula here is of course correct. He says that the sacraments "confer grace in (or by) signifying it (*significando*)"; or "confer the grace which they signify" (*cf.* Denz. 849). The two constitutive elements are present: grace and its visible signification. But the emphasis placed on the one principal verb "confer" may lead one to think that the main aim of the sacraments is to confer the grace of God exclusively, and that the accidental and secondary manner in which they do this is, in fact, by signifying it. It was undoubtedly with some awareness of this possible misinterpretation (SC 62) that Vatican II strove to bring out both aspects (*cf.* SC 59).

12. "The way in which Christ manifested his will in this regard may have differed from one sacrament to another, and as a matter of fact cannot be discovered with certainty for all of the sacraments. His will did not need to be expressed with explicit clarity, for there is such a thing as an implicit, unparticularized, but nevertheless real manifestation of will. . . . This makes it clear that even in the more explicit institution of other sacraments by Christ the fundamental institution of the Church, as the sacramental saving sign, remains the essential factor. For as we have seen, this fundamental institution of the mystery of the Church is an implicit institution of the seven sacraments. And perhaps this implicit institution is the only manifestation of Christ's will regarding one or another of the sacraments—matrimony, for example" (Edward Schillebeeckx, *Christ, the Sacrament of the Encounter with God*, Eng. trans. New York: Sheed & Ward, 1963, pp. 116–118).

13. What is more, the latter would be strongly conditioned by the needs and obligations of occidental society assimilated to the life of the Church. For centuries sacramental practice and civic participation would be practically synonymous. The moral code fashioned by theology as the requisite for sacramental practice would owe much more to civic morality than to the exigencies of the gospel.

14. The Church does not consider herself to have power to change the "substance" of the sacraments which she received from Christ. But this is affirmed of those things which, "according to the testimony of the fonts of revelation, Christ himself instituted" (Denz. 2301). The preciseness is significant.

15. *Cf.* Volume I, Chapter III, CLARIFICATION IV.

16. Hence it is not this feature that must be modified or reformed in the sacraments (*cf.* SC 67, 71, 72, 77, etc.).

CLARIFICATIONS

I. TRUE EFFICACY OR EFFICACIOUS TRUTH?

People used to talk about the "efficacy" of the sacraments and they still do. A "valid" sacrament is an efficacious sacrament.

What relationship does this efficacy have with other efficacies we know and deal with: technological efficacy, political efficacy, the efficacy of love in history?

This is not a theoretical game of concepts. To prove it we will begin by asking a few questions that are rarely brought up in connection with the sacraments.

Among Latin American Christians we have seen the spread of antidevelopment positions, which have been all but officially sanctioned.[1] This outlook does not stem from contempt for development. It represents a refusal to fall into the trap of conceiving underdevelopment as merely backwardness in the whole march toward the "integral development of man"—an expression that is now rather threadbare and worn.

When underdevelopment is pictured as tardiness or backwardness, we are offered formulas which "technical experts" picture as being endowed with some kind of automatic efficacy. They are, as it were, the *rites* of development. Their scant visible efficacy contrasts sharply with the confidence placed in them and with the restrictive way in which they are imposed.

To put it another way: Aren't the technocrats a class of secularized priests, just as priests seem to be the technocrats of the sacred? And do we not have the same or a similar postulate of authentic efficacy in the crisis of development as we have in the sacramental crisis? Is not the vanguard of Latin American Christians faced with the same challenge in both cases?

If people set up political efficacy in opposition to technological efficacy—the latter being semimagical—they do so because the former seems to be more true and authentic. For it includes two fronts: the struggle to obtain the material goods that are absolutely necessary for a decent human life, and the need for all human beings to participate freely and actively at every level of social decision-making.

This comes down to formulating the conjecture that the context of the sacramental crisis in the affluent world is, at its very roots, quite different from that of more aware Christians on our continent. It may well be that the distinction we made in the previous volume[2]—between the "death of God" as attrition on the one hand, and secularization as taking cognizance of the decisive, sacred value of the secular realm on the other—leads us to this appreciable difference.

In other words: the Latin American believer poses the same "what for?" about his historical praxis and his "sacramental" praxis. He is no longer content to utter the key word: efficacy. He suspects that this term often serves to leave the "wherefore" shrouded in obscurity, when the whole weight of decision should focus on it.

If a person does not recognize that history has its own proper salvific density, that it is a real though imperfect and ambiguous anticipation of the final kingdom, then he will employ the term "efficacy" for activities that have little relationship to the salvation of history. Concerned almost exclusively with what lies beyond history, he will not scruple to talk about an efficacy which leaves the process of history in the hands of what Paul calls "powers and dominations."[3]

In Christian thought any dualism which separates man's preoccupations creates a dangerous ambiguity around the word *efficacy*. For the Christian who is earnestly committed to man's liberation, giving *truth* and veracity to this word means combatting all the residues of dualism.[4] And since this dualism is in practice the deepest root of conservative stances in history, that is to say, since it is profoundly ideological, the question of adopting a unified vision of history and affirming its profound salvific import is not merely a theoretical one. It is a political act in quest of *true efficacy*.

At this point we run into an unexpected convergence which is critical to our theme. If we frame such notions as faith, grace, sin, salvation, and other similar ones within the conception of one unique historical process, then the concept of *truth*—which is intimately connected with faith—cannot escape the same process of re-positioning.

Is it possible for the truth that derives from faith to form a realm of its own, the realm of truth-in-itself, when faith and those other terms are subject to the test of historical efficacy? Must we not end up defining truth as Rubem Alves does, when he says it is "the name given by an historical community to those acts which were, are, and will be *efficacious* for man's liberation"?[5]

In other words, once truth has been introduced of necessity—by God himself—as a dimension of historical praxis on behalf of man's liberation, then it would seem to include *efficacy* in its very essence. If a person accepts divine revelation, he should not be afraid to say: the only truth is *efficacious truth*.

So we may ask: Within the context of a history which is the decisive destiny of all human beings, when is something *true* in a man's life? In a famous talk Cardinal Lercaro said that the freedom to inquire—and hence to make mistakes and correct them—was not a right *in spite of* the right of truth but rather respect for the truth as we encounter it in human life. The truth that man possesses is not the truth attributed to a formula from the outside, which he then repeats. It is the truth we arrive at in real-life praxis, the latter verifying and correcting our knowledge. It is a realm in which the catalyst is none other than efficacy.[6] It is not true, after all, that our deepest and most authentic questions arise from the failure of our praxis to procure for us the satisfaction we expected from it?

Everything we say in this volume about the sacraments will prove to be sterile reformism if it does not get beyond all dualism and question the *true* efficacy and the *efficacious* truth of a sacrament as well as of a political decision.

The efficacy of the sacraments, then, cannot be understood as the efficacy "imputed" to a juridically valid rite (even as Cardinal Lercaro denies the quality of truth to the truth "imputed" to an objectively correct formula).

It demands that the sacraments be historically "true": that is, efficacious with respect to man's liberation in real-life history. In other words, the sacraments will be valid and efficacious, as Christ intended, to the extent that they are a consciousness-raising and motivating celebration of man's liberative action in history. That does not reduce them to a merely human gesture.[7] God is operative in them, but his activity consists in working through the praxis of man. Hence it condenses in the sacramental celebration where man intensifies his conscious awareness of the import and liberative force of his action. Where that does not happen, there efficacious truth and true efficacy will be missing—no matter how perfect the rite is. And hence we would not be dealing with the Christian sacraments.

II. AMBIGUOUS EFFICACIES AND THEIR SACRED PARALLEL

Making efficacy true and truth efficacious is certainly a principle, a central principle, that informs both historical and sacramental praxis. But is it enough to enuntiate this principle? What criticism does it inject concretely into both the sacramental system and historical acitivity?

A Christian community must be attuned to criticism of any and every form of ritualism, whether it be sacred or secularized. That brings us back to the three realms we mentioned by way of example in the previous CLARIFICATION: technological efficacy, political efficacy, and the historical efficacy of love.

1. In sociological terms the affluent societies, which are often called "consumer societies," can also be called "profit societies." To understand what the term "profit" contains, we must enter into a relationship between man and nature and not into a relationship between man and man, for it does not fit in the latter context.

In this way technocracy narrows the concept of efficacy. It strips it of its most important qualitative content (i.e., its ethico-political content) and limits it to its pragmatic, utilitarian content that is measurable by quantitative criteria. For the sake of this "profit," the human being is reduced to a factor that is ultimately extrinsic. The same thing is true in current sacramental concern.[8]

But the framework of developmentalist democracy is even more complex in its ideological aspect and mechanisms. And, as we shall see, it has its parallels with the distorted image of sacramental efficacy.

In the previous CLARIFICATION we pointed out that developmentalism attributes an almost magical character to certain activities, lines of conduct, and socioeconomic processes. It becomes a secularized sacramentalism.

Just as in the case of the sacred rite, people *attribute* an illogical efficacy to a model that is supposed to be beneficial to those "in the process of development" (e.g., the investment of foreign private capital). Just as in sacramental practice, we have a rite which actually is a cult rendered to an interested god. And the god in this case is the affluent group that offers "aid," that appears to be giving when in fact it is receiving.[9] Just as the salvific efficacy attributed to the sacraments masks the loss of time, energy, and historical efficacity, so developmentalist aid maintains in a proletarian status the nations on the margin of the politico-economic empire. They remain instruments, not subjects, of their own history.

In both cases another point is also important. So that no one will make unfavorable comparisions between what is given and what is received, it is important that the author of this "liturgy" belong to a different world. This author must operate outside of historical praxis, where comparison would inevitably crop up. He must promise an invisible efficacy, one that is exempt from the more realistic criteria based on what man wants to achieve with his energy, his time, and his activity in history. The technical expert, like the priest, must be a-political.

Obviously it is difficult to determine what is cause and what is effect in this marked convergence. Let us simply say that, at the very least, a human life imbued with the prevailing conception of the sacraments prepares us to accept the same mechanisms on other levels of existence. It is the same dualsim that paves the way for ideological a-politicism on the part of both technological experts and priests.

2. When we use the term *political* here, we are not alluding to the makeup or support of a specific party. We are using it in a more general way, referring to the dimension of the *polis*, to the construction of the "city of man" that is part and parcel of every human project that manages to evade the magic spell of profit. Politics presupposes an analysis of existing society in which the "wherefore" always takes priority and precedence over the "how." In other words it is an analysis in which the fundamental question is not how to make society function but how to make it more humane. Thus the political dimension coincides with the ethico-historical character of man's activity.

It is certain that this dimension fashions a loftier plane of activity than one which is subject solely to profit. But this does not mean that the criticism framed in terms of political efficacy is in fact free of ambiguities. It too evinces ambiguities that parallel the ones we have observed in the ordinary conceptions of sacramental efficacy.

The first notion of efficacy associated with the political realm is the notion of maintaining order with the least possible measure of violence. "No political regime has found a definitive solution to the contradictory demands that the government be *wise* on the one hand and yet rise out of *popular consent* on the other. All existing regimes represent one possible compromise between these two exigencies . . . A functional democracy is one which has found ways to give people the *impression* that its rulers are carrying out their will, while making it possible for the rulers to make wisdom prevail."[10]

Now to convey this "impression" which is essential for the maintenance of the system, it is necessary to carry out certain rites that manifest the power at the disposal of the people who, in another sense, are kept as subjects: i.e., as people ordained principally to obey, to be part of an order fashioned by others (whether their dominant quality be wisdom or greed).

These rites are often the rites of formal democracy, especially in the affluent society. Where want is more evident, on the other hand, it often happens that political efficacy looks for more powerful rites. Dictatorships are capable of displaying spectacular achievements, and of inculcating a powerful instinct of guilt in those who do not opt for communion in the order that makes it all possible. Often this blind feeling of guilt is the only political "participation" of the masses in the order that decides their lives.

In the Church the sacraments have served to generate a similar idea of ecclesiastical efficacy. Rites—and those in charge of them—resolved conflicts by setting up a "magical" kind of participation. Meanwhile, decisions were made by those who had control over the rites. At the beginning of this century Pius X, in his encyclical *Vehementer*, wrote in terms that suggest a political parallel: "The Church essentially is an unequal society. That is, it is a society formed by two categories of persons: pastors and flock. . . . As far as the multitude is concerned, they have no other duty than to let themselves be led."[11]

The political phenomenon of "populism," so common in Latin America, and its own peculiar efficacy display a marked convergence with the prevailing image of sacramental efficacy.

Populism frequently sets itself up in opposition to the existing order, in the name of the people. It is the *native* representative of the people, taking them as they are and representing them as such. In their natural leaders the people do not see people who represent a profound awareness of social conflicts. What they do see are people from another world of power and know-how who perform the magic rites of sympathy, camaraderie, service, and hope. Thus they fashion a visible bridge between the masses and power. They are "pontiffs," that is, "bridge-builders."

With them out front, the crowd does not have to make conscious the mechanisms of its oppression. It does not have to explicate and express, slowly and painfully, its own word and its own latent conflicts. The rites dispense it from that process—however little they, for all their magic, get close to the people's feelings, language, and temporal pace.

Who does not see that a certain "populism" informs liturgical renewal when it does not get beyond the point of making the faithful accept rites as *their own* natural and spontaneous expression of their yearnings? Is this not the case with discussions that try to operate with the faithful before and *about* the sacraments. Like political populism, do they not leave untouched the real problems of people, which are certainly there but which do not find their way into awareness, word, and action?

Here again it would be superfluous to explore which sacramentalism, the secular or the religious, gives rise to the other. Once again the important thing is that the mental outlook which makes one possible also opens the door to the other. And, on the other side of the coin, a dialectical and critical outlook in one realm spontaneously combines and grows with the parallel outlook in the other realm.

3. The ambiguities of technological efficacy and political efficacy turn us back to the Christian question *par excellence*: the efficacy of love.

But we cannot allow ourselves to be deluded in this matter. Talking about the efficacy of love does not automatically solve anything. Its efficacy is subject to the same ambiguities and competes with the same oversimplifications. True and efficacious love is a complex reality.

To begin with, the choice between love for all and love for some is a complicated matter. Today we are often told that Christian love is a universal love. Oddly enough, however, the means offered to us for carrying out this love could never achieve universal dimensions.

The language of the gospel, mirroring the problematic and the social structure of an epoch, talks about love in terms of interpersonal attitudes and encounters. But if we continue to talk about love in the same terms today, in the face of the socialization process that is taking place in world history, are we not simply evading the issue (GS 30)?

The "sacrament of brother" is often spoken of today as a micro-process of interpersonal encounters. But neutral as it may appear, is it not in fact a rejection of the broad historical perspective opened up to love by the great human questions of our time: hunger, poverty, domination, etc.?

We often find in ecclesiastical circles a great concern for the fact that large social structures do not leave any room for "Christian love." These circles want to have enough free time and space to resist the crush of socialization. They want time for counsel, almsgiving, charitable works, prayer, worship, the sacraments, etc. And it is certainly true that if human activity does not take account of the personal dimension and its intense moments of signification, intimacy, and commitment, it will often end up looking for a love that is efficacious only in terms of profit.

But this threat of dehumanization should not lead us to dissociate these "intense moments" of personal life from the global process of historical liberation. The Christian sacrament is not made for our "spare time." It is a rhythmic, dialectical dimension of societal and historical activity. It is the community's way of reactivating and deepening our interpretation of, and commitment to, the historical process geared toward man's liberation.

III. THE EX OPERE OPERATO MAN

If a person reads the conclusions of Trent attentively, he will understand something that should be evident from the gospel itself: that *ex opere operato* effectiveness is not a feature of the *rites* employed with the sacraments but of *grace*—or, what comes down to the same thing, of God. So we get a contrast between two aspects of the sacraments: (1) insofar as they depend on God; (2) the fact that grace is received only "sometimes" and by "some people" (Denz. 850–51).

On the level of his divine relationship with us, God infallibly repeats what he carried out in the act of *creating*. His word and his will have no limits or obstacles. We are the new creation, and we are it just as we were the old: *ex opere operato*. The only thing is that in the new creation, where our liberty finds its absolute—supernatural[12]—dimension, the power of God stops at our door and calls out. Grace is not capricious. It is there, whole and entire, at the disposal of those "who do not place any obstacles" in its path (Denz. 849).

This gives rise to several questions that are profoundly related to the life of the Church. Whence the privileged status of the *seven* sacraments, if they do not constitute the only way in which God's grace acts *ex opere operato*? Does it make any sense for us to have in fact given them such a privileged position? And if we have valued them excessively, what aspect of ecclesial practice has been hurt in the process and how much? Has it perhaps been our commitment to transforming the face of history?

The hypothesis that the grace of God, whole and entire, is available to men at every moment of their existence is really more than a hypothesis. It is a certainty. But if that is the case, then it is just as certain that human beings have countless signs to recognize it (at the same time they receive it). As we saw, the Church never said that the sacraments are seven *because* only on these seven occasions does grace work with a special efficacy.

Let us assume that grace and signification—the latter being part and parcel of Christian (or ecclesial) grace—come together on innumerable occasions. To be more precise, let us assume they do every time that man sets himself to the great adventure of gratuitous giving and to the great battle of life against death. What is to stop us from recognizing countless human signs as sacraments? Nothing, from the viewpoint of the relationship between grace and sign, but a great deal if we take into account the communitarian function of the sacraments.

Friendship, for example, has countless signs in which to express itself. So does conjugal love, and commitment to man's liberation. All the realms of love call for the creation not only of new conditions but also of new signs. And yet they keep going back to the age-old ones, not because they are old, but because they are universal.

The seven sacraments are precisely seven because they are signs which, balanced by the necessary creativity and relativity, constitute the Church as a universal community. They have the disadvantage of entailing a certain routineness and a basic a-temporality if they are taken in isolation from a creative community that keeps fashioning new signs; but still they serve to instruct, question, and commit the Church in its totality. They bring the solidarity of a common quest to people who are living through different and even radically opposed situations and challenges. They ensure that each individual base community in the Church will not escape into an over facile and uncritical unanimity in its response to a specific urgency.

In a Church that is alive, the seven sacraments constitute a fountainhead of conflicts, not some goal of security that is attained in spite of the divisory elements. They are not meant to submerge and quench conflict in uniformity.

Once again the essential thing is that the sacraments are meant to point a finger to the function of the Church, rather than the Church pointing toward them. But this shift suggests another parallel one in our conception of the minister of the sacraments. In general, this is the priest (to use a word that seems highly improper to us, for reasons we will discuss later).

The priest is associated with the idea of ritual efficacy. Without him the effect of grace in the sacraments would not take place. Grace would not flow. A layman can repeat the words of consecration over and over again, but nothing would happen! Nothing really important would happen, no matter how much fervor, commitment, and improved faith would be invested in the ceremony.

To put it in other words, words which we hate to admit, we picture the priest with magical powers. But if that were the case, there would be no sense to the condition that the Church has traditionally imposed if the action of the sacramental minister is to be valid.

After all, what intention does a magician have to have to produce his magic effect? Either all or none. Either he must will concretely to obtain what the rite is aimed at producing, or else the rite itself—observed with formal exactitude by someone who has the power—is valid and efficacious by the simple convergence of its material elements, even though the magician's mind may be elsewhere.

Now sacramental theology seems to stand somewhere in between these two poles. And its stance, precisely because it has nothing to do with magic, has given rise to much discussion and debate. When ministers are performing and conferring the sacraments, they are required at the very least to "have the intention of doing what the Church does" (Denz. 854).

The only coherent interpretation of this requirement voids the classical magic hypotheses.

Doing what the Church does, as we have already noted, obviously means putting the sacraments in the service of the function entrusted to the Church. It means making them serve ecclesial purposes. It means making them point up the specific mission of forming a community and leading it to its commitment in history.

Outside of this function the sacraments are devoid of meaning. For either they are the tools of egotism rather than grace; or else, lacking signification, they will be a point where grace comes to man without the connotations that make it *Christian* grace—i.e., grace destined to fashion a community and prepare it for its mission.

Thus the objective intention of the minister to do what the Church does is not an idle question for specialists. It is a question that challenges the whole existing sacramental system of the Church. For it calls into question the very nature and end of the Christian sacraments such as they are now received in most cases (SC 62).

If what we have said is true, two conclusions follow. And they point up two inescapable tasks facing the Christian community.

1. There must be a living, creative, functional balance between the seven universal signs whereby the Church recognizes, lives, and questions itself as something universal, and the significative creativity required of each particular Christian community as it confronts and celebrates its commitment to human history.[13]

But just to give serious consideration to this balance, we Christians must free ourselves from the bank-account attitude toward the sacraments. That is, we must stop regarding them as seven privileged rites which provide us with a way to ensure our own salvation. If our outlook does not change in this respect, the whole realm of signifying grace in a creative way will remain unexplored. Significative creativity will always take second place to the sign considered as something efficacious independently of the needs of the community. We will not waste time and energy on "secondary" matters when we think that the essential thing is obtained by mere repetition of "the seven sacraments."

The Church must be free enough to formulate a correct sacramental approach. And to do this she must take seriously the obligation of doing "what the Church does" in the sacraments. She must reverse her order of priorities. The sacraments are made for the Church, not the Church for the sacraments. How difficult this change can be is something we have already indicated in our discussion of the relationship between rite and security.[14]

2. The second consequence may be even more critical, since it is more deeply imbedded in the institutional structure of the Church. It has to do with the function of the minister of the sacraments.

If his presence is not magical in nature, if his powers are not indispensable for grace (and hence salvation) to come through the rite, if on the contrary his presence is required in order to "do what the Church does" with the grace that God sends to it, then we must radically change our idea about him.

Vatican II repeatedly gives us orientations in this new direction. To begin with, it deliberately restores to the "priest" his quality of being a "minister." In the terminology of the primitive Church, he is a "helper" who renders a service. There is no little importance in this step, which more or less "desacralizes" someone who seems to perform a ritual, sacred act and who therefore is placed in a position of being served more than in a position of serving, by virtue of his sacred powers.

Even more important is a second step, which injects even more concrete content into the first step and moves even further away from a *sacred* interpretation of the minister. That sacred interpretation is found imbedded in the term "priest," which is certainly not evident in the primitive Church. Following the lead of the primitive Church, Vatican II again designates the minister of the sacraments with the original Greek term *presbyter*. This term can be translated "elder," but it is more comparative in connotation. The *presbyter* is the older person who takes charge of a particular group and presides over it. This does not mean he manipulates it. In this context it means he gives the community what tradition confers on it. It means relating it to the other existing community groups through something which always has to be substantiated and actualized in local situations but which is never exhausted in any one group: i.e., through something that transcends them.

It is important to note that Vatican II disregards the notion of a vertical relationship between "priest" (someone endowed with certain powers) and "people" (those in need of these powers). Instead it stresses a communitarian function: "The office of pastor is not confined to the care of the faithful as individuals, but is also properly extended to the formation of a genuine Christian community. If community spirit is to be duly fostered, it must embrace not only the local Church but the universal Church" (PO 6).[15]

So the sacerdotal function is not a magical one. But this should not make us think that the priest can be replaced quite naturally by lay people who may be better prepared than he is. The institutional need of a visible community means that roles cannot be interchanged —not even by way of exception—simply because at a given moment someone is more capable of exercising a function.[16] The same applies to any institution.

IV. OTHER "MAGICS" IN CHRISTIAN LIFE

Our consideration of the *ex opere* man should help us to realize that the aura of magic is not associated solely with his *sacramental* function, but with his whole ministry.

In our ordinary use of language we associate the concept of magic with the concept of superstition, and we relate both to visible expressions of ignorant, primitive religiosity.

The witch doctor of a savage tribe comes closest to our conception of magic. As civilization progresses, magic in that sense recedes into the background. It comes to mean the primitive traces remaining in a culture that is no longer magical. It means the isolated superstitions of a rural area or such phenomena as astrology and horoscopes in urban areas.

After the wave of antireligious attacks in the last century, it seems we have reached the point where superstition and magic are terms no longer applicable to the classical forms of Christian sacramentality in the West. But this view of the matter is a vast oversimplification.

Accepting this state of affairs on the level of language usage, Church renewal directs a critical eye toward certain marginal aspects of our "religious life" and remains unperturbed about the rest of it. But the whole problem of the "magical outlook" is much more extensive, deep-rooted, and complex. For magic is not simply a matter of *being mistaken about the procedures that might possibly have divine efficacy.* If it were, we could easily distinguish superstition from sacramental practice in *a priori* terms. But magic is a matter of looking for divine efficacy in certain procedures without any relation to historical efficacy.

In the last analysis, magic is the absence of historical realism. It is invoking a-historical powers to solve the problems of history. So magic is any and every procedure which rejects the criteria of historical causality because it sees them as merely human and sees God as someone who operates through other mechanisms that are known only to the initiate.

At this deeper level, sacramental practice can be just as magical as "superstitious" practice. When Paulo Freire labels the nonawareness of the oppressed as something magical because it is ingenuous, passive, and nonproductive, he is using the same notion of magic that we have just described. To say it again: it is not the religious mechanism employed that determines whether we are dealing with a magical attitude or not.

Such a magical outlook is just more clearly evident in the crass forms of superstition. For in them we see that the world is divided into two levels with their own distinctive efficacies. On the one hand there is the real world, whose mechanisms of domination man does not dare to attack; on the other hand there is the world of nonnatural explanations which enable us to evade reality and leave it as it is.[17]

We know that the sacraments lose their real nature when they lose
their inner relationship with faith (SC 62). But does not faith itself lose
its real nature when divine revelation or dogmatic formulas are accepted
in such a way that they do not lead us to solutions that are "fully human"
(GS 11)?

Vatican II admits that many Christians, being derelict in their education about the faith, obscure rather than reveal the authentic face of
God and therefore are more than a little responsible for the rise of
atheism. Now this is not due to the fact that they depart from strict
orthodoxy. They do not obscure the authentic face of God simply because
they ignore the trinity of divine persons or the unity of the deity. Nor
is it due to the fact that they ignore the infinite power and perfection
of God. In other words, they can be "orthodox" and still obscure the
face of God!

So we may well ask: Whence comes the importance that is attached
to the fact that the Christian stay firm in his orthodoxy, that he not
accept (for example) three gods and one person, since he may still be
denying God for all his orthodoxy, sincerity, and reception of divine
grace?

The answer is clear. The importance that is ordinarily attached to
formal orthodoxy is magical in character. Here again historical efficacy
is replaced by efficacy of another type. Even though we do not see
historically why three persons and one God has more efficacy than three
gods and one person, the importance of the first formulation resides
in the fact that it is considered to be *directly* associated with salvation
by God. Any orthodoxy that does not essentially point toward orthopraxy
is magical.[18]

That is why the Church is often content with a blank-check approach
in practice. The faithful sign their name, and it is up to the Church
to fill in the exact formulas of faith and what they mean. But what efficacy does this blank check have? None but a magical one, since people's
ignorance of its content means that it has no historical consequences.

And so we get the small, or radical, contradiction that remains to
be overcome, even in such documents as those produced by the Medellín
Conference. Once we show that salvation does not just refer to some
transformation of man in the hereafter but also to his total liberation
from bondage in history, then we must also say that this also obliges
us to "historicize" the notions that form the content of faith for the
faithful. If we do not do this, then we are giving with one hand and
taking away with the other.

Here is just one example of what we mean. If salvation consists
in man's liberation in history and metahistory (GS 39), then this presupposes a God who is profoundly interested and involved in man's history.
But if we present God as some inaccessible being who is perfectly happy
in his infinity no matter what happens in history, and what is more,
as someone who kindly makes contact with man not in the space and

time of history but in some separate, detached, cultic locale, then we are offering a magical escape-hatch to Christians. And this image will speak much more forcefully to them than any episcopal document will.

But it is not just dogma that injects an aura of magic into Christian life, however civilized the latter may be. Our moral teaching can be seen in the same light.

We show our thanks to God by "doing what he wants us to do." The statement and formulation seems to be correct. Indeed it seems to suggest real commitment and involvement in history. After all, didn't the prophets use God's demands for justice to prevent cultic worship from giving false and artificial tranquility to people who were using it to opt out of history and feather their own nests?[19]

Well, reference to an already established law can only have liberative import in two very special contexts. Firstly, when it gives expression to attainable interests that are loftier and more communal than those which prevail in ordinary life. Secondly, when it effectively points toward a future that is still to be reached but that can be glimpsed in outline. That was the case with the law invoked by the prophets.

In most cases, however, the law expresses precisely the opposite. It inculcates conformity, based on abstract and atemporal considerations, with some *status quo* created to benefit very special interests.

This feature of historical evasion is accentuated by cultural and social mobility. As it becomes advantageous and even necessary to replace "natural" possibilities with new artificial possibilities, and as new images of societal life show up on the horizon as possible replacements for those which seemed to have stemmed from nature itself, a law that supposedly was sanctioned by God ahead of time increasingly shows up in its true light: i.e., as an evasion of history. And like every evasion of history, it is magical.

If we say we possess an instrument of moral orientation that is already finished and perfected independently of the concrete needs of the people and the society around us, and if we say that this instrument is backed up by God and endowed with decisive efficacy for salvation, and if at the same time we cling to an atemporal model of moral living, then we are engaging in a typically magical procedure.

A similar statement could be made about the very structures of the Church, about the way we comprehend and exercise the magisterium, about the way we orient our pastoral effort, and much more. So the sacraments are far from being the only elements in Christian life that are jeopardized by the magical outlook. The central concern of this whole series has been Christian liberty and its involvement in history; that is, the conquest of such magical elements. But it is undoubtedly in connection with the sacraments that the magical alternative shows up most concretely and tangibly, together with its underlying mental structure and its full consequences.

NOTES

1. *Cf.* Medellín's document on Pastoral Concern for the Elites, MED II, 127–136. Even more forthright is the article by Bishop Eduardo Pironio (the Secretary-General of CELAM, "Teologia de la liberación," in *Teologia* 8 (Buenos Aires, 1970): 10

2. *Cf.* Volume III, Chapter III, CLARIFICATION I.

3. In Volume V we shall try to show that the angelology present in Paul's writings has a political point, even within the context of his own thought. And it is this fact that justifies our use of his words here in a common, present-day sense.

4. See Appendix II in this volume.

5. "Apuntes para una teologia del desarrollo," in *Christianismo y Sociedad* 7 (Montevideo, 1969): 27.

6. In explaining why tolerance is, paradoxically enough, more related to respect for truth than to respect for freedom of opinion, Cardinal Lercaro has this to say: "What are we to say of our moderation in this whole question? Is it just pragmatic clear-sightedness into the present historical situation, in which we cannot bring the heretic to the stake? Or is it based on loftier principles such as respect for truth, or even for God's activity in souls? We prefer to say that it is based on *respect for truth and the human way of arriving at it* (*Documentation Catholique*, 1959, col. 337 ff.).

7. This was what Trent condemned—rightly or wrongly interpreting the sacramental theology of Protestants in this sense.

8. Indulgences would be an extreme case of profit applied to the supernatural realm. But the sacraments themselves—with their notions of requirements, efficacy, and frequency—bespeak a similar outlook. They are viewed on the level of a man-thing relationship. Their practice would be fundamentally different if they were viewed in terms of a Man-men and a men-men relationship. But if we look at things realistically, and consider one concrete example, what religious congregation would agree to replace its half hour of daily Mass with an alternation between shared words one day and Eucharistic liturgy the next?

9. The Brazilian newspaper *Correio da Manhã* reported a conference between the Brazilian Minister of Foreign Affairs and German businessmen in its issue of March 13, 1969. He told them that "due to the deterioration in the exchange rate, in the period from 1954 to 1966 Brazil had lost five billion dollars on its exports—a loss that was greater than all the foreign aid received in the same period."

10. Raymond Aron, *Dix-huit lecons sur las société industrielle* (Paris: Gallimard, 1962), p. 89. See also pp. 87–88 in the same book.

11. Dated February 11, 1906. One might think that a lot of water had flowed under the bridge since then. Yet, even though it does have a different idea of the laity, *Lumen gentium* often tends to define the laity as mere receivers of the sacraments (*cf.* LG 13, 31, 37). Only an overall vision of the Church in the world situates the laity in terms of its central and specific function rather than in terms of the sacraments (LG 36).

12. Speaking of *two* creations, like speaking of the *supernatural*, can have the negative effect of dissociating two elements that are meant to form part of one and the same process. But this logical distinction is required for an understanding of the gospel itself (GS 22 and 39). See also Volume I, Chapter I, CLARIFICATION II; and Appendix II in this present volume.

13. See Chapter I, CLARIFICATION III.

14. See Chapter I, CLARIFICATION I. Here we can bring up events and facts that have stirred debate in the Church in recent years. We refer specifically to the celebration of the Eucharist by members of different Christian confessions. General debate has centered around the question of whether or not such a celebration is really the Eucharist. And that question has hinged on whether and how the Catholic minister has participated in it. With such a formulation of the question one is still operating out of a semimagical perspective wherein the Christian community is made for the sacraments. To the extent that we discover again the community that unites us with other Christian confessions, it seems logical to share the same privilege with them if we operate out of that perspective. This is true even if one has doubts whether all are dealing with the same thing.

If, on the other hand, the sacrament is made for the real community and fashions it into unity, then unanimity of faith is its logical component and presents a far greater obstacle to sharing the Eucharist with people who do not share the same faith than do the invalidity of the rite or the absence of a Catholic minister. In other words, Eucharist and oneness of faith mutually affect one another, when one does not picture the Eucharist as merely a religious rite.

But even here we are faced with another question. We do not know whether the Christian "community" which receives the Eucharist nowadays possesses this unanimity merely by virtue of its confession of faith. Or, at the very least, we do not know whether this homogeneity is as great as that which often unites members of different confession in those decisive points where faith is verified in commitment to history and thus achieves its aim.

15. *Cf.* PO 10; LG 28; and Medellín's document on priests, nn. 16 and 21 (MED, II, 178 and 180 which (like LG 20) stresses that bishops and priests have received not the ministry of the sacraments but the "ministry of the community."

16. Concerning the preparation of the minister for the exercise of this function, see Chapter IV, CLARIFICATION II.

17. Here again we can quote Marcuse's commentary on Freud's remark that Christians are "badly christened": "They are 'badly christened' in so far as they accept and obey the liberating gospel in a highly sublimated form—which leaves the reality unfree as it was before" (*Eros and Civilization*, New York: Vintage books Edition, 1962, p. 64). On the topics tnat follow see Segundo, *De la sociedad a la teología* (Buenos Aires: Carlos Lohlé, 1970), Part II, Chapter I.

18. See CLARIFICATION I in this chapter.

19. "Although they ask counsel of me day by day and say they delight in knowing my ways, although, like nations which have acted rightly and not forsaken the just laws of their gods, they ask me for righteous laws and say they delight in approaching God. Why do we fast, if thou dost not see it? Why mortify ourselves, if thou payest no heed? Since you serve your own interest only on your fast-day and make all your men work the harder, since your fasting leads only to wrangling and strife and dealing vicious blows with the fist, on such a day you are keeping no fast that will carry your cry to heaven" (Isa. 58: 2–4).

CHAPTER THREE

Sacraments That Speak

If what we have been saying is true, the Christian community as a whole is a sign. And the content of that sign is at once an historical event and the structure of any and all human progress: i.e., the paschal mystery of Christ. That is the fundamental dialectic that underlies the whole process of evolving love between human beings.

What is more, this dialectic does not simply *take place* in us; it is also shown to us by the signs we call sacraments. And it is shown to us so that the ecclesical community may contribute what is specifically its own to the construction of human society: i.e., what it knows, what has been *signified* to it.

Hence the sacrament is dialogic. It prepares the Christian community to speak its liberative word in the history of mankind. Obviously enough each generation of human beings faces different problems. But our faith tells us that they share a common denominator: a death and a resurrection, a death for a resurrection.

All progress stands bewildered before death, which seems to close off the road ahead. Individual human beings and whole peoples experience it. Death is difficult to accept because it does not hold any certainty of resurrection. Resurrections are always discrete. And they almost never seem to be directly related to the gift of self that was the death which preceded them. Only much later, and in very broad outlines, does the historian manage to relate one thing with the other. And even that does not always happen. It is certainly not the case with the life of each and every individual or group.

God's revealed word gives us a "yes" answer to the question. It provides us with the certainty that our hearts are looking for but which is not given by events themselves.

Yet within the infinite variety of situations in which the question of death and resurrection crops up for each new generation, certain key moments do seem to reappear where the questions evince similarity and convergence. They are key moments for every generation even though the questions may vary from one to the next.

We could say that they are the moments in which the life-denying forces, the forces of death, gather together and become visibly tangible, forcing crucial questions on man even though he may be inattentive to what is going on in his own life or the lives of those closest to him. Let us look at these key moments.

1. The moment of birth is one of these key moments. However paradoxical it may seem, it is a moment when we can clearly see the forces of death surrounding the spark of new life. Hence it is a moment that makes man ponder a great deal, and with good reason.

At birth a human being is so defenceless and fragile that only human society can save it from death. But that brings us to the first and fundamental question: Does society want this new human being? Does it not consider the newborn infant a threat, especially if it is born into the world of the poor? Would it not prefer to explore outer space and walk on the moon than to put its resources at the disposal of this little creature, perhaps born out of misjudgment or ignorance or ill will?

This life-denying force, rejection, is only one of the forces of death. If the infant survives rejection, it will still have to confront other obstacles that are even deeper and more structural. It will have to turn egotistical and hardnose to elbow its way into a society based on egotism. And in that society it will constantly have to choose between killing or being killed, between exploiting others or being exploited by them.

What signification and import, then, is there in living before the specter of a death that is already operative, and that has dimensions as broad and as deep as the world and heart of man?

For us this signification is bound up with a positive response. Our response does not ignore the life-denying forces nor does it let man evade their death-dealing power. But it does assure him that there is a force for life by which death will be overcome. This life-affirming force is the fact that there is a love waiting for him, a love which is that of God himself. This love will give the new being a life of its own so that death may be converted into definitive resurrection. And the Christian community commits itself to converting this love into an historical reality, into a transformed society, into a leaven of resurrection.

2. Another key moment in man's life is the painful and controverted appearance of liberty in adolescence. In every generation adolescence has posed serious questions to human beings. The question is not so much what the adolescent will decide to do with his liberty, what he will make of his life with it. It is rather whether his liberty will be able to make its way through the structures of biological, psychological, and societal life

which not only ignore it but positively combat it. May we not say that the adolescent is the clearest embodiment of the divided being which Saint Paul describes—one torn between his ideals and dreams on the one hand, and what reality permits him to carry out on the other? The forces of death confronting this inner man are a society that ignores him and imposes its impersonal structure on him; a law of minimum effort and least resistance which causes him to slip unwittingly from love into egotism; and a terribly powerful foundation where the unconscious joins with societal imperatives to turn him into just another object.

Here again the answer comes from divine revelation, and it says yes to man's expectations. It is signified by an anointing which unites person and destiny and gives strength and a vocation.

But here again it is true that this destiny and this vocation do not escape liberty's clash with structures. They do not even avoid defeats. But out of these defeats there rise life and liberty, because these latter realities are supported by an incomparable force of resurrection.

3. The next key point is not so much a moment as a question. It is the question about the duration, permanence, and solidity of real community between human beings.

Long ago Saint Paul pointed out (1 Cor. 11: 20–21, 29) that the acceptance of inequality is a death-dealing force for any group of human beings that wishes to form a body, that is, a community. In the course of its life a community is jeopardized by everything that gives one man the advantage over his fellow, by everything that converts someone into a passive object rather than a thinking subject in the group.

But perhaps the greatest threat facing any community is that of routine. It is jeopardized by the law of minimum effort and its consequences, which gradually replace the earnest inner contribution of each and every person with the strong and difficult bond of merely external union, with the laws of mere coexistence, and with the ceremonies that caricature real love.

We must not think that this death can be avoided. The real question is whether the community can recover after this demise. And to answer this question Christians receive the grace that makes communitarian love possible, with a sign of the unceasing resurrection of the love that knits the community together.

The Eucharistic sign drew from our human experience one of the most extraordinary and almost miraculous tokens of a community in which love returns to life every day: the family meal, the communal food table which does not depersonalize the participants but rather signalizes a singular and irreplaceable locus to each one of them.

Clearly enough this is true in most cases. But is there any human sign that cannot be vitiated by egotism? And of all such human signs is this not perhaps the one which in most cases and in the best way signifies the daily resurrection of love above the chains of inequality and routine?

4. Intimately connected with the communitarian "moment" is another moment which can properly be called such. It is the moment of rupture or breaking with the community. The forces of sin (that is, of disunion) can grow slowly and unnoticed. But there comes a moment when consciousness forthrightly accuses a man of having broken with the community and its function. Or what is worse: of having broken and destroyed the community itself.

All sin is a precipitate synthesis of elements focused around oneself. It is a synthesis fashioned without going through the work of accepting others and making them a part of it. All sin is anticommunitarian even though it may proceed from some love. For in this case love has been narrowed down and made easy. It has been converted into the denial and rejection of a more broad-based love, a more service-oriented love, a love more deeply rooted in real liberty.

The consciousness of having destroyed some possible love or some possible community raises one of the most agonizing questions in the life of each human generation.[1] Once man realizes that all love, all community, all group-life is based on the most delicate, dynamic balance, the corresponding failures weigh more heavily on him than death. Is it possible, after all, to refashion a love that has been undone?

The Christian response is a clear "yes." But it does not indulge in any illusions or unreal optimism about the easiness of this restoration. The realization of having destroyed some possible love should not cause man to succumb to the weighty burden of his culpability. But it should bring him to a *metanoia*, that is, to a conversion in which resurrection follows the voluntary acceptance of one's death, one's separation from the community denied. This sign of death and resurrection is precisely what takes place in the sacrament of penance.

In penance God does not just exercise his power of pardon. This pardon is signified by one's reintegration into the community after the separation brought about by sin. This separation must take exterior form— vis-à-vis the Eucharist—so that God's response may be seen as explicitly signified. His response is a life-giving force which reintegrates the community and which turns sin itself (and its consequent death) into the pledge of a new community of love. What is more, there is no human community whose creativity does not derive from this resurrection and from sin (in a negative but real sense). No love progresses without death and resurrection, without sin and reintegration.[2]

5. There is almost no need to point out that the moment when two beings join together intimately and totally for the rest of their lives has always raised a profound question in man's mind. It is perhaps more true of this moment than of any of the moments discussed so far, even though—or perhaps precisely because—every generation sees the happening repeated and witnesses its difficulty and its frequent failure.

The forces of death threaten the life and the real love of *every* community, as we noted above. Hence they also threaten the life and love of this "specialized community" which, according to Paul, suggests the union of the Church with Christ. Like the latter community, the matrimonial community has its own death-dealing force. It is the same force that gave rise to it: i.e., sexual attraction.

To be sure, this attraction does not consist solely of a instinctive and material force that brings two beings of the opposite sex to encounter and satisfaction. Starting from this base, sex gives total shape to a human being, affecting even his moral and spiritual features.

But is it possible to shoulder this dimension freely and convert it into a gift without reservations or evasions when it is precisely this same dimension, with all its depth and power, that can give rise to egotism as well as love, betrayal as well as fidelity, and routine as well as creativity?

The Christian response, signified in the sacrament of matrimony, is certainly not a legalistic one: i.e., that marriage is indissoluble. It goes much deeper.

Eros, the attraction, ought to lead to *agape*, the gift of self. But it is not just a straight-line path, a moving ahead, an evolution. It is also a death. The "old man" of Saint Paul (Eph. 4: 22–24) is precisely our old human nature that allows itself to be carried away by the impulse with which love began. However, this impulse must die in order to reach its real terminus: the "new man." By passing through this daily death of the purely instinctual, *eros* becomes *agape*. It turns into a love that is capable of building something definitive and eternal.

It is a difficult death indeed, for it does not consist in ridding oneself of the sexual as of some evil. It consists in turning the sexual into something personal, intimate, and dialogic so that it may rise again as a deep and profound union.

6. The sacrament of orders, more than any other, would appear to be incapable of any connection with a profound question related to humanity. After all, is it not an anointing that turns a man into an intramural servant within the Christian community?

But the breakthrough of imperious communitarian exigencies into a life where love seemed to have already fashioned its course has always been one of the most profound questions faced by human love. Just above we saw that sex, taken first in its narrow, instinctual sense and then in a broader spiritual sense, constitutes the normal opportunity, source, and force for man's self-giving. But this normal course does have, not an obstacle, but an alternative. The community to which a human being belongs, above and besides the community of the family, often confronts man with total demands that exclude or at least jeopardize the specialized community founded on sex and parenthood.

The worker who accepts responsibilities in the cause of unionism often realizes that he is condemning his family to perpetual instability and even, perhaps, to poverty. The same holds true for the honest politician who feels called to consecrate his life to transforming the society in which he lives. In short, if someone accepts the summons and need of the community in its totality, he knows that in most cases he is shifting the greater part of his life outside the samll community of marriage and family where love is more restricted and limited on the one hand, but also closer, clearer, and more satisfactory.

Clearly this is the source of one of mankind's most profound questions: To what extent can we "burn our bridges" in love?[3] To what extent can social responsibility, when accepted, be turned into real love without the understanding and support and satisfaction of a group that is indeed small but also more affectionate? To what extent does this love for "the many" go, without turning into a lust for power and a political egotism that replaces a more intimate and personal love?

Christian revelation gives a positive response to this question, saying that it can be done. In a symbolic gesture, it entrusts the Christian community to the love of a man even as a wife is entrusted to her husband in a key scriptural text on marriage (Eph. 5:25).[4]

We could say that all human love, and the paschal mystery that it embraces, is framed between these two poles: i.e., between the death and resurrection signified by marriage, and the death and resurrection signified by ordaining a man's love for a community.

7. The forces of death are certainly most visible at that moment in life which, for the Christian, is connected with the anointing of the sick.

It is not so much because this anointing signifies the proximity of physical death, or its certainty. Rather it is because sickness, especially sickness which robs man of activity and places him passively in the care of others, brings with it a profound question: What can a love that is merely passive do? What use has mere resignation to one's own suffering? Even more pointedly, what use is mere resignation to the suffering of others, to the suffering caused by necessary care and by the passivity and uselessness itself?

The Christian response is nothing else but the paschal mystery itself.

This involuntary and painful passivity, this death accepted, becomes itself an active instrument of love—either because health returns, or because death this time signifies one's real and definitive resurrection from the dead.

The victory of love over death, or over passivity which is its analogue, causes the community of the faithful to congregate around the sick person as one who, here and now, is positively constructing the definitive body of Christ.

And so from birth to death the Christian is associated through each sacrament with the perennial questions of humanity. And along with the communitarian commitment of his gesture he receives the response that God sends to those questions: the surety of victory over all the types of death that go to make up the life of man.

NOTES TO CHAPTER THREE

1. The whole play of Jean Anouilh, *Traveler without Luggage*, deals with the condition of the human being who cannot divest himself of his past and who therefore carries it around like a dead weight throughout his life. By contrast, the amnesia of the protagonist seems to give him the chance to be the only person who is able to realize the *dream* of everyone. But even this exception is illusory, as we discover during the course of the play. The past returns to demand its due. Even when one starts over from zero, one is enmeshed in the past and its guiltiness. As Valentine says: "Listen, Jacques, you really will have to give up this wonderfully simple life of yours. It's too easy to live without a memory. You'll have to accept yourself, Jacques. Our entire life, with our fine moral code and our precious freedom, consists ultimately in accepting ourselves as we are. . . . Today you've come of age. You're about to become a man again, with everything that entails in the way of failures and blemishes—and moments of happiness too. Accept yourself and accept me, Jacques" (Jean Anouilh, Eng. trans., *Plays*, New York: Hill and Wang, 3 volumes, 1958–67, III, 163).

2. In his booklet *La Misión de la Iglesia en una sociedad socialista: Un análisis teológico de la vocación de la Iglesia cubana en el día de hoy* (Matanzas, August 1965), Sergio Arce Martínez, professor of systematic theology in the Presbyterian Seminary of Matanzas, writes: "For the Christian, work is an expression of the communitarian destiny of humanity. . . . Thus the Christian in his work labors with the intention of cooperating with God in incorporating humanity into the kingdom. . . . An aside is in order here, because one cannot help but note the irresistible power of the socialist moral code on occasions insofar as it relates to performing one's duties to society. Here there is no point of transcendental support, and this results in the problem of *pardon for sins.* I am not referring only to pardoning others but also to the experience of feeling oneself pardoned. . . . I think that if there is some value in Christian witness in connection

with this communitarian and societal effort, it resides in no small measure in the experience of pardon. One of the things that move me most deeply is the fact that honest men, dedicated Communists, and upright citizens have ended their lives, literally or morally speaking, because they could not withstand the irresistible power of the socialist moral code."

3. In the verse which the poetess Idea Vilariño composed for the popular song *Guantanamera*, we hear a man saying goodby to everything he loves in life as he prepares to go off and join the guerrillas. Although he does not want to leave his wife and mother and loved ones, the oppression of others must come before his own loves: "Adiós, linda, no me llores / dejo todos mis amores / que me llenaban la vida / dejé a mi madre querida / y a mis hijos los dejé./ Dejo todo lo que amé / por irme pa' la guerrilla./ Ya me voy, ya me estoy yendo / tal vez no te vuelva a ver / mucho te supe querer / pero, mi vida, yo entiendo / que la angustia y el dolor / la opresión y la miseria / de los pobres de la tierra / están antes que mi amor."

The last months of Che Guevara's life loom in the background of the poem. He often brought up this dramatic problem facing man: "At the risk of seeming ridiculous, I must say that the true revolutionary is guided by great sentiments of love. . . . This may well be one of the great dramas confronted by the leader. He must combine a passionate spirit with a cool mind, and he must make painful decisions without twitching a muscle. Those in the vanguard of revolution must *idealize* this love for the people, for the most sacred causes, and make it *one and indivisible. They cannot descend with their little dose of daily affection to the places where the average person exercises it*" (cited by Nils Castro, "Che y el modo contemporáneo de amar," in *Casa de las Américas*, year 10 (1970), n. 58, pp. 124 ff).

4. *Cf.* CLARIFICATION III in this chapter.

CLARIFICATIONS

I. INFANT BAPTISM: IS IT STILL MEANINGFUL?

The baptism of newborn infants has always been a thorny problem in sacramental theology. Even though there was no lack of explanations and images at the popular level, it continued to be an alarming exception on the level of dogma.

Vatican II says that the sacraments "not only presuppose faith, but by words and objects they also nourish, strengthen, and express it" (SC 59). Logic would demand that we begin that statement instead with "some sacraments" or "most of the sacraments" or "all the sacraments except one." It would seem to be a simple replacement at first glance. But in fact it would oblige us to alter the overall conception of sacramentality that we have been expounding so far. For the fact is that at least one of the sacraments seems to have a purely magical nature. It does not presume anything personal in the subject, and it radically alters his destiny through persons, events, intentions, and rites that are alien to him. And if this is true of one sacrament, why not of all?

The Council of Trent declares: "When the Apostle says that man is justified by faith, this statement must be understood in the sense that has been maintained and expressed by the perduring and unanimous feeling of the Catholic Church—viz., it says that we are justified by faith because 'faith is the principle of human salvation' (Saint Fulgentius), the foundation and root of all justification, without which it is impossible to please God and enter the consort of his children" (Denz. 801). Once again logic would require more traditional theology to correct this statement and substitute very different phrases. For example, it would be obliged to say that for at least ten centuries faith was the principle of salvation for only a small minority of persons. For if we take due account of the high infant mortality-rate, at least more than half of those "saved" were saved by a baptism received before any faith was possible for them.[1]

In other words, the classic theology was fashioned on the basis of the adult—or, at the very least, on the basis of a human being endowed with reason and liberty. As far as the baptism of newborn infants was concerned, it simply alluded to the exception without integrating it into its theology as a normal case.

In raising the problem of the baptism of children who have not reached the age of reason,[2] however, we do not do so because it constitutes a special difficulty within our conception of sacramental theology. On the contrary, we feel that the theological coordinates proposed in this volume enable us to understand what is happening in the baptism of infants, and even to justify this seemingly odd practice of the Church over the course of many centuries.

To some extent the baptism of infants sums up in brief the major themes we have been discussing and developing.

1. Baptism ostensibly gives to the Christian child what God gives to all children: birth into a redeemed world, that is, participation in the liberation which Christ brought to the world (GS 2, 19, 22).

This means that with respect to man's fundamental situation vis-à-vis sin, death, eternal life, and a future liberation, baptism does not set up two groups of opposed human beings by virtue of some magic applied from the outside.

So one has no grounds for arguing that baptism should be postponed until the child possesses reason and liberty, so that it may freely decide whether it acknowledges the (privileged) reality that baptism affords it. For this "privilege" does not exist to begin with.

Nor, on the other hand, does one have a right to argue the other extreme. One cannot say that since this is the most decisive option in life, and since it does not require faith or liberty in the child but the simple application of a rite, it is a Christian obligation to apply it to any and every child no matter what the faith and will of its parents might be—just as one tries to save a defenceless being who is in danger of death. The Church has felt and openly indicated that this is not the case (cf. Denz. 1489, 1490, etc.), thereby giving implicit but clear testimony that it does not consider the choice between baptismal *rite* or no baptismal *rite* as the sole or decisive factor with respect to salvation for infants.

2. Baptism constitutes the *sign* of a grace that all human beings receive at the moment they are born into a world which could have been a world enslaved to the powers of death and destruction but in fact is not. Because grace abounded even more than sin did, it is a world where love and life triumph so long as they are not opposed by man's free and express will.

Christians do not have a monopoly on grace, but they do have a monopoly on its sensible, significative, sacramental manifestation. And it is precisely this (objective) significativeness that increases to the extent that the sign is connected with the human moment that the grace relates to: i.e., man's birth into a redeemed world. That is why the baptism of a newborn infant is something which better signifies a reality that is mysterious to the rest of mankind but patent for Christians: i.e., that the victorious forces operating on the new temporal and historical exis-

tence of this new member of the human community are the forces of
love which liberates history, thanks to Christ.

The only thing is that here we run into two objections. The first
objection is that in this case there does not appear to be a situation
of (original) sin preceding grace,[3] as was the case when it was assumed
that sin and the devil ceded their place at the moment when baptism
was conferred—and only in the event that it was conferred. Among
the things in favor of this objection is the way in which the Christian
ritual expresses itself. In particular it is supported by the exorcisms,
the phrases designed to expel sin and the devil so that their place in
the soul of the newborn may be occupied by God and his grace.

Just as we should not minimize this argument, so neither should
we confuse the role of imagination and the role of reason in explicating
the data of faith. The fact is that such words as *redemption* and *salvation*
assume that the grace of God repairs a situation where man finds himself
faced with radical impossibility. And here the ritual tries to help us
to *imagine* this change by presenting us with the successive presence
of Satan and then of God.

From the viewpoint of theological reasoning, there is no need to
imagine such a succession. The idea of redemption presupposes a *logically*
prior situation of enslavement, even though man is in fact born
redeemed, even though God is the first "inhabitant" of this being. For
if God is the first inhabitant, he is so as a liberator, as one who repairs
a situation that would have been the reality *necessarily* if redemption
had not taken place.

Only thus can we understand why the Council says that God gives
all men some way of associating themselves with Christ's paschal mystery
(GS 22). If there were a *moment* subsequent to birth at which redemption
overcame sin, and if it only took place at that moment, then not *all*
those who found themselves between birth and that moment would
have the possibility of associating themselves with the redemptive mystery.[4]

But that brings us to the second objection. If that is the case, one
might object, then baptism *doesn't change anything*.

One could say in reply that the gap between the grace received
outside of the baptismal sign and the grace received in baptism measures
the distance that separates the vocations of men of good will from the
vocation of one who is a member of Christ's visible Church with its
own specific mission and exigencies.[5]

However correct this response may be, it does not suffice on the
plane of classical theology. For we must get down to the level of language
usage. In the objection cited above, the term *baptism* is used as a synonym
for the sign, independent of the grace that it signifies. But in prevailing
theological usage, which has little concern for pondering what is going
on in the extraecclesial sphere, the term *baptism* (like the names of the
other sacraments) includes in its connotations not only the *sign* which

belongs to Christians but also the *grace* signified (which is not conferred only on Christians).

Thus Trent hurls an anathema at the person who says that "Baptism is a matter of free choice, that is, not necessary for salvation" (Denz. 861). When we read these words, our first impression is that Trent is talking about the liturgical rite which we call baptism. But Trent is applying the term *baptism* primarily to *the grace which is proper to baptism*, that is, to man's participation in Christ's redemption. Only secondarily is it applying the term to the rite. So true is this that Trent declares (Denz. 796) that the *desire* can replace the rite. Obviously enough it is not desire for the rite. Here desire means the good will of the person when he sincerely desires what the grace of God gives—whether it be in the signified form of a sacrament or in a manner "known only to God" (GS 22).

That is enough to solve an important matter of language usage. All the declarations about the absolute necessity of the sacraments refer to "sacrament" as it is understood by theology. That is, they refer first and foremost to the grace which is conferred and signified in it. The necessity of a sacrament insofar as that term includes the rite is always relative to a person's situation. That is, it presupposes faith and, along with that, the conviction that the proper responsibility of the Christian includes living out grace on the level of conscious awareness and dialogue.

3. Hence we hold that grace, which is absolutely necessary for salvation and which consists in an inchoative participation in the redemption effected by Christ, is given to all human beings; and that in the case of Christians, and in accordance with their specific function, it is accompanied by a sign. We also hold that this sign shows up all the more clearly, the more connected it is with the human moment in which this participation not only takes place but also serves as a response to one of the great questions facing human society: in this case, when a new member of the community is starting its life.

But that confronts us with a new problem: When baptism is conferred on a newborn child, is not the gain in objective signification matched by a corresponding loss in the area of conscious awareness?

This question, which sounds quite logical to us at first hearing, is typical of a certain mental outlook that we have already analyzed. We tend to assume that the sacraments are conceived for the sake of the individual. To us the existence of a Christian community merely seems to be a prerequisite—nothing more—for the individual to be able to receive the sacraments he needs for his salvation.

We do not consider the fact that the sacraments are destined for the community itself even though, in terms of signification, they refer to key moments in the life of one or more community members. They are made so that the grace conferred may structure a community by way of signification; so that it may be turned into a community; and even more specifically, so that it may be turned into a community that thinks and dialogues in terms of what is really taking place in history, above and beyond mere appearances.

Clearly enough this presupposes quite a radical revision of ecclesiastical practice. The sacraments are and should be communitarian happenings and not an individual relationship between recipient and minister (the latter being God's substitute) such as they are today even in group ceremonies. Baptizing a group of infants at one time does not turn the event into a communitarian happening. To be a communitarian happening there must be a living community which commits itself to the task of discovering and communicating its import, as we indicated in the main article of this chapter.

It is precisely this which justifies the baptism of newborn infants. It is a secondary matter that only after some years will the infant come to a realization of what is signified in the sacrament: i.e., a grace which does not separate him from other human beings but rather unites him with them and orientates him toward them. But it is important that the Christian *community*, and in particular those entrusted with the education of this child, grasp the elements which revelation and history combined together offer them for that task.

That is precisely why the normal practice of the Church is to confer baptism only when there is a presumption that those entrusted with the care of the child will shoulder the commitment to educate it *in the faith*. And educating it in the faith means gradually and progressively showing it reality as the Christian sees it with the help of revelation.

4. But at this point we face another problem. We move from the *new* objection that baptism does not change anything, to an old objection that is just the opposite: i.e., that baptism unduly or excessively changes the existence of the chold.

We may readily acknowledge that baptism does not determine the being or destiny of the child independently of his personal decision. But from a psychological and sociological standpoint it would seem that we affect it even more by committing a community to educate this child *in the faith*.

There has existed, particularly in the last century, a laicist conception of liberty and what it should be. It opted for a total liberty, so that a human being would be "free of all prejudice" and a *tabula rasa* when he or she reached the age of being able to decide their personal destiny. This idea of liberty is totally illusory. The values that are the indispensable basis for willing are discovered by guided experiences. No one would choose to study, for example, if he could spend his life playing; if the experience which study gives were not guided energetically by an older generation which recognizes value in it. And no one would claim that it is desirable for a human being to arrive at the age of eighteen completely ignorant, but "free" to choose education or not.

However, there are some people who would grant this example but not others, because they feel that there is no introjection of values and "prejudices" in education. But let us suppose the case of a person who arrives at the age of eighteen without having had the experience of family life and what in theory are its limitations. This person also has not had the experience of generous sharing and solidarity. Now these experiences are not something we have chosen. They could be called "prejudices" because they are exercised without one's being able to establish why they are preferable to egotism and promiscuity. Yet who would say that our hypothetical person of eighteen is really more free because he has not gone through these experiences?

The Christian community does not commit itself to bring the baptized infant to faith. It commits itself to bring the child to liberty,[6] introducing it to its specific value-experience which corresponds to the baptismal sign. Only much later will the child freely accept, reject, or rectify this kind of experience. To imagine that liberty would be much greater without these values that are grasped empirically is not a theological error. It is a psychological and sociological error.

So far we have presented our theme here by posing and answering objections. That may seem to distort the proper balance, suggesting that we are trying to justify a practice which common sense tells us we ought to change.

Phrased in positive terms, however, our position is that the baptism of infants is or should be our way of experiencing—first as a community and later as individuals—one of the greatest questions in human life. Here the question is localized in a concrete history, and we experience God's answer to it. His answer is that all human beings are born into an already liberated world, which should be liberated even more by the power of love. Living through this experience in baptism, the Christian community pledges to turn it into a dialogue with the rest of mankind.

II. SACRAMENTS AND SOCIETAL INFLEXIBILITY

In a time of change such as the Church is now living through, it is interesting to note that the most immutable realm is not that which derives from dogma but that which derives from the sacraments. We are referring to situations associated with the sacraments of matrimony and holy orders: divorce, birth control, the marriage of priests, etc.

At first glance it might seem that we are exaggerating the disjunction here. After all, the opposition to divorce and remarriage seems to derive from Christ's own message: "What God has joined together, man must not separate."[7] Nevertheless in "Christian" countries this situation seems to be presented only in the sacrament and by the sacrament. The fact is that we do not consider that God has "joined together" baptized people who went through a civil ceremony of marriage, however deep and real their love might be. After countless marriages of this type, it is still acceptable to break the civil bond and the existing familes in order to celebrate a sacramental marriage. Only then do people come under

the norm: "What God has joined together, man must not separate."
Thus, in the life of the formally baptized Christian, the solubility or
indissolubility of marriage depends on its sacramental celebration. So
the situation does not stem directly from the Christian message but
from a specific sacramental theology.

A similar statement can be made about the opposition to artificial
methods of birth control. It is presented as deriving from natural law.
But in fact it stems from a specific conception of the ends of marriage.
This has been especially true since the pill came into use, for one can
no longer use the argument about the destruction of life.

By the same token we know that priestly celibacy, which is not based
on some legality associated with the sacrament of orders, is indeed
associated with its significative essence.[8]

What are we to think about all this in the light of our presentation
of the sacraments as signified and consciousness-raising grace? The
answer is not simple. And the course we must adopt to take a stance
will serve to shed light on some of the fundamental elements of sacramental theology and its revision.

The Church is not the ideal image of the world. It is not the world
as it ought to be. It is the community—just as human as any other—which
possesses and is obliged to transmit elements of a solution that were
revealed by God and that are addressed to the historical problems of
mankind as a whole.

As Vatican II pointed out, this does not mean that the mere application of divine revelation to history contains the ideal solution for which
we are looking in the concrete. It does mean that this application should
be considered as one of the data that will enable us to arrive at solutions.

What we have said does not free the Church from the necessity
of organizing itself as a community in order to effectively transmit the
message which has been entrusted to it. Societal visibility is indispensable
to the Church. But buried within this visibility is one of her most acute
and dialectical problems.

The fact is that effective communitarian transmission implies the
visible translation of the message into communitarian attitudes. This
is not grounded in any triumphalist aim. It is due to the fact that the
Christian community transmits its message in words, and inevitably they
will be referred to its attitudes and interpreted in accordance with them.

Hence the Church is obliged to determine concretely the compatibility
or incompatibility of attitudes and lines of conduct with the message
she is supposed to transmit. She does not do this as if she were the
first to come along and decide what would be the best legislation binding
on all citizens. She does this as a community endowed with a specific
function and hence confronted with equally specific needs and requirements. By the same token, however, in this functional and inescapable
communitarian visibility are buried certain ambiguities that often con-
verge to dilute its impact.

For one thing, *social* visibility cannot be individual; by which we mean that it cannot take into account all the concrete circumstances of each case, which are often inner, psychological circumstances. What is involved here is a structural visibility. In other words the lines of conduct which it assumes to be suitable for transmitting the message should be comprehensible by virtue of a certain conformity.

Without a doubt there will be different lines of conduct which individual circumstances will explain and justify even from the viewpoint of the Christian message. But if, without any possible explanation, they were placed on the same level as the normal line of significative conduct, they would destroy the signification of the latter as well.

Thus the functional visibility of the Church is of the external, legal order. This means it must allow for ambiguity, but not for pharisaism. We get the latter when the functional judgment is presented as God's own judgment on the person in question. We also get it when some exigency in the significative and legal structure allows an even greater countersign to exist along with it.

Let us take the question of marriage as an example. Let us agree that the gospel does not seek to add new concrete prescriptions to the law but rather to bring the law to its fulfillment, proposing the new law of love as the one commandment. If we agree on that, then we must also agree that the comments about remarriage, offering the other cheek, and plucking out our eye if it is a source of scandal point toward new possibilities and fulfillments for love; they do not seek to increase the number of moral commandments.

Love, promised forever and offered at all times, is to be understood as offering the other cheek when one is struck. This is in the nature of a proposal of creative love by Christ, *which does not judge ahead of time whether this is the best solution* in each particular case posed to love. In fact the only time that the gospel mentions Jesus getting struck on the cheek, it does not say that he offered the other cheek. It says that he asked to know why he had been struck.

So what are we to say about the indissoluble character of marriage? Is it a situation that should be repeated automatically in all cases of marriage, whereas offering the other cheek would be judged by the criterion of love's efficacy? Everything in the gospel disproves such a dualistic interpretation.

If we do not accept such an interpretation, then we must conclude that the indissolubility of marriage is a concrete application of a central point in Christian revelation: i.e., contrary to all appearances, no love is shipwrecked, no love is in vain, no love is lost.

One's belief that he can entrust his whole life to the totally fulfilling—even though invisible—power of love is the thing which makes it possible for him not to enter a new union which would shortcircuit the possibilities of a love given forever to someone who is still alive. So we can see that indissoluble marriage is not simply a law which the state would do well to impose flatly on each and every one of its subjects, whatever their beliefs might be. It is not an "ecclesiastical law" that ought to be translated automatically into "civil law."

But when the Christian community lives love in this way and commits itself to it, it is transmitting part of its message. The message would be useless if attitudes did not give meaning and realism to the words. In other words, it elaborates a concrete strategy within the overall function of the Church.

The term *strategy* might appear to be excessive. But we must keep in mind the fact that in the burgeoning Christian community there did exist a very concrete, situation-oriented strategy for signifying the message of love in a communitarian way. If, for example, the Church recognized indissoluble, monogamous marriage as an exigency of its own communitarian life, it did so because the society in which the Christian message was born and spread *already was* a monogamous society. Within this structure the Church sought to manifest, in its attitudes, possibilities that went even further than what was being done in reality.

On the other hand, this same society was one that had slaves. And the same Church which judged monogamous marriage to be a "natural" exigency of love, did not judge the obligation of actually liberating slaves to be equally "natural." Here too the signification of love was made manifest in a visible exigency: slaves were to be treated well. But this visible demand was understood within the coordinates of the society it knew. Someone who bought or sold or had slaves could belong to the Christian community.

This shows that the *functional* visibility of the Church does not proceed from some sort of a familiarity with an immutable natural law. Instead it is really rooted in the significative variations of existing society within the Roman Empire.

But the Roman Empire was not the whole world. When the Christian message reaches countries where the normal societal structure is polygamous, it may well not be aware of what its *functional* visibility is as yet. It simply transposes the requirement of monogamy, which was significative in a different social structure.[9]

If Christianity had arisen in these societies, it might perhaps have ruled out slavery (which was part of the great empires) but not polygamous marriage. At least it would not have ruled out the latter immediately, that is, so long as other elements in the structure did not undergo change. It would have considered polygamy as the "natural" expression of love.

Now one might claim that polygamy makes a woman into a slave. But some of the members of the early Christian community were real slaves, and the Christian community did not demand that their masters liberate them.

This discussion might appear to be rather purposeless and byzantine. But let us translate it to the societal structure of the Latin American continent. As we all know, in middle-class circles the renunciation of a second marriage during the lifetime of one's spouse, based on the belief that love never suffers complete shipwreck, does have significative value.

But at this point we must ask ourselves two fundamental questions. Does it have the same significative value in other social situations that are not those of the middle class? And even if it does, is this signification balanced by the other aspects of the Christian message?

For example, does it signify efficacious love among the Latin American proletariat where the mother, abandoned and left with children to care for, is unable to make justice prevail in her favor on the one hand, or to care for the needs of her family by herself on the other because woman's work is not priced in those terms? In the eyes of those who know and appreciate that situation—i.e., the vast majority of Latin Americans—is it a sign of love or of egotism for her to look for someone to care for herself and her children by means of a new union that will not be sacramental, or legal, or perhaps even lasting?

And, on the other side of the coin, is the exclusion of this immense cadre of mothers from the Christian community a *balanced* sign of the Christian message, so long as continuing participation in that community is afforded to those who help to keep this societal structure going—by their sins of omission at the very least?

If the sacraments are to contribute to the creation of a community that signifies or makes transparent a message, then it is necessary that the commitment which they presuppose be accepted with the full burden of its visibility—but also with the full functionality of a message that is to be transmitted in its complete and perfect sense. In no case should it be transmitted as a divine judgment on persons.[10]

III. SACERDOTAL CELIBATE AND HUMAN CELIBATE

From the previous CLARIFICATION it is evident that it is illusory to look for a law which is independent of space and time in order to establish the exigencies which correspond to the sacraments. Their organization into something concrete and visible is functional. Their criterion is the efficacy of the community's transmission of the Christian message.

In contrast to the question of marriage, the Church does not presume to link celibacy and priesthood in terms of natural law. It admits that it is a functional matter. Insofar as the supreme hierarchy is concerned, however, it does not show any willingness to cast any doubts on its functionality.

By the same token, if the sacrament of orders is not the transmission of intraecclesial magic powers, if it is instead the sign of a response given by God to a much broader question that concerns all humanity, then the functionality or nonfunctionality of priestly celibacy cannot be treated in terms of pragmatic convenience either. We cannot decide the issue solely in those terms: e.g., as the solution to the crisis in religious vocations, or as a way of multiplying base communities.

The universal Christian community commits itself to transmit a message when it celebrates a sacrament, for the sacrament is the visible sign and response to some great question of human existence. So we must ask here: Does the celibate have a relationship with the communitarian visibility of this message? If he does, what exactly is it?

The only thing to remember is that this question is not one that stands outside circumstances of time and place. Not long ago the bishops of Uruguay quite rightly pointed out that the celibate does not have the same signification in the context of an affluent society that he has in the context of an exploited society such as the one in Latin America.[11] Focusing our attention on that latter society, let us get back to the human question that is bound up with the ecclesial sign of "sacerdotal" orders.

In a society where "institutionalized violence" reigns, as the Medellín Conference pointed out, any societal transformation calls for hardnose commitment to reality. One does not have to be a sociologist to know that one of the greatest obstacles to such commitment, in the area of labor unionism or politics for example, is posed by man's defence of a love that is more concrete and closer to home and that is being jeopardized: i.e., his love for his family.

When any sort of blow is permissible, leaders know that the greatest difficulty in enlisting support for the cause of justice does not come from individualistic or egotistical fear. The most feared blows are those which threaten to strike down the most defenceless sector of a man's life: his family. Commitment to the struggle for justice will commit them as well.

Belief in love is a key point in the Christian message. As John puts it: "We have come to know and believe the love which God has for us" (1 John 4:16). So one of the most evident signs of the Christian message is the formation of a family without any reservations or limits. By the same token, there is another sign that is *complementary* to that one: out of love, a man may "sacrifice" his family and its just interests for the sake of a love that is directed toward the liberation of a whole society.[12]

Now if we believe that this latter kind of love is possible, fruitful, and adequate as a human vocation, then we must ask a question: What will the Church do to visibly express this universal element of her message, which is most pertinent in the present-day life of the Latin American continent?

To begin with, one cannot deny that this exigency is intimately related to one of the sacramental signs, however vague it may be in our reflection. If holy orders is not designed simply to perpetuate the ecclesiastical organization, if it is meant to signify some element of the response that God sends to *all human beings* through the Christian community, then the question at issue must concern a love that directly assumes the responsibility of caring for the whole community.[13]

If this is the case, celibacy and orders, quite independently of the concrete form they take, are essentially united in an intimate relationship as far as signification is concerned. And if they are, they are because "celibacy" (that is, the sacrifice of familial love) and social commitment to justice and liberation are intimately united on the level of signification.

Now someone might say that human beings manage to love society effectively even though they must sacrifice the efficacy of their familial love *partially*. That is certainly true, but it is not an argument against the signification of total celibacy. For celibacy is not a critical judgment on other attitudes, it is a message made visible in a specific attitude. The possibility just mentioned above does not prove anything against celibacy any more than the possibility of fashioning a second fruitful marriage proves anything against the indissolubility of Christian marriage. The possibility is a real one, but the sacramental exigency does not cease to be significative on that account.

So we would say that there is a similar significative relationship between orders and celibacy. But clearly that statement is not meant to decide what concrete form the Christian community should take to make this relationship functionally visible. The Catholic Churches of the East, for example, do affirm this relationship. But they express it visibly in a form whereby marriage is possible for someone before he receives priestly orders. In what, then, is the relationship made manifest? First of all, in the fact that the exercise of orders is not interrupted by marriage. Secondly, in the fact that the more total forms of consecration to the whole community are reserved to celibate priests.

Even in the Western Catholic Church itself, all the distinct grades of orders include a certain consecration to the community, but only one excludes matrimony. When the Church contemplates the important role that deacons can carry out in present-day ecclesial life, she may perhaps be concerned more about preventing the essentials of the sacramental function from being performed by noncelibates than about the real-life needs of Christian communities, in which the Eucharist is as necessary as the explanation of the gospel.

Thus, making visible the relationship between celibacy and consecration to the community is a functional matter. And the relationship itself holds true even on the human level.

But this functionality has a second feature. As we said above, it does not represent a judgment that family life and social consecration are incompatible. Now we can also say that it must be integrated into a complete communitarian testimony. In other words, priestly celibacy will be devoid of signification so long as the harsh requirements and creative risks of commitment are not visibly related to the priest's role. That is why Latin America may have a better chance than other parts of the Church to discover the visible relationship between priesthood and celibacy, as a theology of liberation immerses the priest in the exigencies and dangers of the concomitant commitment. Celibacy and bureaucratic priesthood certainly have no relationship through which the Christian community might be able to make its message visible.

The work of the priest must be seen as an exercise in the insecurity of continuous creativity vis-à-vis the historical problems which the Christian community is, or should be, living through. The work of the priest must be seen as the exercise of the prophetic character of the Christian message against any and every established, sacralized order—be it the repressive order of underdeveloped countries or the contented exploitative order of affluent societies. If the work of the priest is not seen in this light, then the basic problem will not be to eliminate a sign that no longer has any signification. It will be to restore its exigencies to reality. Only then will its signification be discovered anew.

The relationship between priesthood and celibacy is more visible *today* in Latin America. But we are not presenting it as a regional necessity. We are presenting it as a worldwide necessity, which is more recognizable in those places where the Christian community is confronted more inescapably with the concrete consequences of its own destiny.

NOTES

1. *Cf.* Denz. 796 and 798.
2. We realize that one pastoral approach today favors postponing baptism until it can be comprehended as a sign by the recipient. We could go along with this outlook and thus eliminate the difficulty, without going against dogma (see Denz. 866–870, where *other* reasons for postponing baptism are rejected). We also realize that practical pastoral reasons may advise such postponement, especially in secularized, superstitious, or atheistic milieus. But here we are treating the topic solely from the viewpoint of sacramental theology.
3. This topic will be treated extensively in Volume V of the series, entitled *Evolution and Guilt*.
4. Hence Schoonenberg is quite right in saying: "We have explained St. Augustine's opinion so extensively because until our times the conception of original sin in the theology of the Catholic Church . . . is undoubtedly dominated by Augustine. *That image has been corrected only in a few points.* . . . This is most manifest with respect to *the punishment of original sin in children who die without baptism.* True, Augustine's position that nobody can enter eternal beatitude even if burdened only by original sin is still accepted, and rightly so" (our italics; Piet Schoonenberg, Eng. trans., *Man and Sin: A Theological View*, Notre Dame: University of Notre Dame Press, 1965, p. 153).
5. *Cf.* Volume I, Chapter III. Support for this point can be found in the practice of the apostolic Church. It recognized *the active presence of the Holy Spirit* in people by means of the charisms that followed upon evangelization and faith in the gospel. Nevertheless it still went on to confer baptism on these people. The gesture would have been senseless if it was meant to replace the devil's presence with the presence of God. See Acts. 10: 44–48.
6. *Cf.* Volume II, Chapter I, main article and CLARIFICATION V.

7. With reservations (*cf*. Matt. 19:9) that continue to be the object of theological and historical investigation. See for example, V. J. Pospishil, *Divorce and Remarriage* (New York: Herder & Herder, 1967).

8. *Cf*. Paul VI, encyclical *Sacerdotalis coelibatus*.

9. Even if it had been persuaded of the superiority of one structure over the other, the efficacy of love would have required that one start with in-between actions—such as treating slaves well in Roman society—thus seeking to attack the bases of the social structure and not simply to sanction its consequences.

10. *Cf*. Volume I, Chapter IV.

11. "We are convinced that in expressing our line of action we are not only being faithful to the gospel but also responding better . . . to the situation of our own Latin America." (Declaration of April 14, 1970, reproduced in *Vida Pastoral*, n. 18, p. 6).

12. It is worth noting that in the tradition of the Old Testament the *prophetic* vocation is linked with a weakening of the family structure, precisely for the sake of the critical proclamation of the prophet. At times this weakening comes down to the pure and simple absence of a family, indicated to the prophet by God: "The word of the Lord came to me: You shall not marry a wife; you shall have neither son nor daughter in this place" (Jer. 16: 1–2); "Lord, thou knowest . . . see what reproaches I endure for thy sake . . . I have never kept company with any gang of roisterers, or made merry with them; because I felt thy hand upon me I have sat alone" (Jer. 15:15–17). See also Hosea 1:2 ff. and 3:1 ff.

13. So we see from this that we cannot go along with an old line of argument. The relationship between celibacy and marriage is not equivalent to the old dissociation between supernatural and natural. One cannot say that the priest does not have time or opportunity or vocation for marriage because he is occupied with the supernatural, or because the supernatural demands some special "purity." Both sacraments, matrimony and orders, relate to the two poles of a love that is equally supernatural; and both are tied to the same polarity that is inherent in all efficacious human love.

CHAPTER FOUR

A Community in Dialogue

What we have seen so far raises a new question that is very logical and of great practical import. Is it not possible for this whole mystery of death and resurrection, associated with the plane of life's key moments, to be known and lived in dialogue with faith alone? Is the sacramental gesture necessary as well?

After all, it is a classic human experience that repetition of a gesture on the one hand and creativity on the other do seem to be opposed. So would it not be better to live the dialogic content of faith—the paschal mystery of life as a whole and all its moments—without the routine repetition of the gesture?[1]

Despite the pertinence of this question, it does not stem from a pristine situation. It stems from a gesture that has become old, and it asks what we are to do with it. So we should start off with the group function of a gesture that is new, fresh, and significative. Let us go back to the source, in theory at least, and see what we find.

Section I

The fundamental presence of Christ in his Church, of which his *real presence* in the Eucharist is only a function, is what he proclaims with these words: "Where two or three have met together in my name, I am there among them" (Matt. 18:20). "I am with you always until the perfection[2] of the world" (Matt. 28:20).

Now in the general terminology of the Bible, and particularly in the terminology of the New Testament, being gathered together "in the name of Jesus" does not refer to the mere fact of two or three people getting together to invoke the name of Jesus or call themselves "Christians."

In the language of the Synoptic Gospels, the *name* and *kingdom* of Jesus are synonymous (*cf.* Matt. 19:29 and Luke 18:29); and they designate a happening and a task in history. Note this parallelism, for example:

"Thy name be hallowed, thy kingdom come, thy will be done" (Matt. 6:9 ff; Luke 11:2 ff.). When Jesus proclaims throughout Galilee that "the kingdom" is at hand, he describes it not only with deeds (Matt. 11:5) but also by applying to himself this passage of Isaiah: "The spirit of the Lord is upon me because he has anointed me; he has sent me to announce good news to the poor, to proclaim release for prisoners and recovery of sight for the blind; to let the broken victims go free" (Luke 4:18).

When the scribes and Pharisees commit blasphemy by attributing Jesus' works to the devil, the Synoptics indicate that we must distinguish between pardonable and unpardonable blasphemies. That is the view they attribute to Jesus. Not recognizing and acknowledging the "Son of Man" in the ambiguity of history is one of the pardonable blasphemies. The unpardonable blasphemy is independent of one's religious position. It consists in *not going along with* God's intention and will (or spirit) to win domination over the dominator, strip him of his weapons, and "divide his spoils" among the dominated (Luke 11:22; *cf.* Matt. 12:22–32).

This is the absolute option, the authentic collaboration with Christ. And it does not rule out the fact that this collaboration may be realized on different levels of conscientious awareness. When Jesus speaks only in parables to the multitude and then later explains them in private to his close disciples, he is affirming that the two groups have a different function with respect to the same "kingdom," that is, to his plan of liberation which coincides with the culmination of the world. To define the specific function of the community fashioned around him, he presents the following dichotomy: "It has been granted to you to know the secrets of the kingdom of Heaven; but to those others it has not been granted. . . That is why I speak to them in parables" (Matt. 13: 11–13).[3]

Even more noteworthy than the dichotomy is the fact that it presupposes a change in God's plan, which had reserved revelation of the mysteries of the kingdom to a specific nation: Israel. Jesus will explain the why and wherefore of this change, thereby formulating a decisive warning for the "new Israel": that is, for his own community, for those who have come to know the ultimate secrets of the kingdom, for his band of "friends" (John 15:15).

In Mark's formulation, the purpose of Jesus' speaking in parables is to *accelerate* the change from one people to the other. In Matthew's formulation, it is just the attitudes that motivate the change which are set forth. But in both cases the cause of the change is clear. The people who had been chosen to give something they knew about have instead held on to it and prevented it from bearing fruit. They have regarded it as their private possession ensured by orthodoxy. So even what they "had" was taken away from them. When they turned truth into their possession, truth itself escaped them. Seeing they did not see, hearing they did not understand (*cf.* Matt. 13:12–13).

It is clear that this is a warning for the Christian community, the new and ultimate addressee of the kingdom's secret—and not just from the obvious context. The Greek text of the New Testament warns us about letting our minds get "fat and flabby" (Matt. 13:15)—that is the faithful translation. If we do this, if we think to "take possession" of something which really has been given to us so that it may bear fruit in a history of liberation, then not only will we not figure out anything from what we have been given but we will also hear without understanding. The truth we have will be in formulas and not in our understanding. And the latter will be "heterodox" in the very moment and act of repeating correct formulas.

Paul explicitly draws this conclusion in his classic image of the olive vine, some of whose branches have been cut off so that new ones may be grafted on to it: "But if some of the branches have been lopped off, and you, a wild olive, have been grafted in among them . . . put away your pride, and be on your guard; for if God did not spare the native branches, no more will he spare you" (Rom. 11:17–21).

This evangelical conception of the Christian community rejects any and all nonfunctional "accumulation" or "piling up" of grace and knowledge in the Church, for it sees this as erroneous and dangerous. In so doing, it brings the sacraments face to face with their true function.

Section II

To adopt an expression used by Paulo Freire, there is no doubt that the common sacramental theology is of the "bank-deposit" type. And it is so in two senses.

First of all, it is so because it communicates something that is assumed to be accumulable. Stress has been put on "frequenting the sacraments" as if failure to frequent them meant failing to collect a grace one could collect. One would thereby accumulate less grace than one could.

The only limitation on this frequentation of the sacraments would be the dispositions required to collect the grace. Right here we find a second way in which sacraments are conceived in terms of a bank account. For these dispositions in fact coincide with the *minimum* requirements for belonging to the established order (both ecclesiastical and social). In other words, one must have minimal membership in the Church in order to obtain and retain what it gives—grace and truth —through the sacraments and magisterium.

As a result one's focus of interest is this. What one obtains from the sacraments is the end. And the means is participation in the religious society, a participation that is ultimately individualistic. Thus here, as in the banking system itself, what accumulates for the recipient also accumulates for the benefit and insurance of the bank too. The sacramental grace becomes a bond that maintains a certain membership in the Church and guarantees a minimum degree of conformity with her.

Thus the proper scale of values between sacraments and community, between the accumulable and the functional, is turned upside down. The Church succumbs to a process of "domestication" which thoroughly negates its liberative commitment to the message of Christ. And this is true no matter how reformed the liturgy may be, no matter how close the faithful may get to the words and gestures—the latter being imposed as direct means of obtaining a supernatural rather than a terrestrial efficacy.

It has been said that the existing process of education is that of the ruling classes, in the sense that it comes from them and engenders conformity with them, depositing in the recipient alien words, gestures, and values instead of stimulating and evoking his own word.[4]

We can say just as well that the existing process of sacramental administration is that of the ruling classes. Words, gestures, and values are deposited in the faithful without any effort being made to have them speak their own word; indeed there is no allowance for that at all. More than anything else in the Church, the sacraments appear to be the *gift* which the "ordained" give to those who are not ordained. And it is not without reason that they take up most of the Church's time. In no way do they appear to be the preparation of the whole community for its interpretative, prophetic, liberative task.

But if we restore these two elements to their proper proportions, what do the sacraments signify? If we conceive and live and reformulate them in function of a community whose liberative action is secular and historical—as the gospel indicates[5]—what would their explanation and their concrete essence be?

We can only answer this question by taking a brief look at the import and signification that gestures have in man's group life. We can go on from there to apply this information to a nascent ecclesial community.

Section III

Rahner starts this analysis with the following statement: "The whole process can be compared to the life shared in common by two lovers. Everything they do is sustained and transformed by this love and is its very discreet, almost imperceptible expression—even the insignificant, ordinary things which seem to have quite a different meaning and purpose from love and which would have to be done even if there were no love between these two persons. And yet, sometimes, and even often, they must tell each other their love openly in words and by gestures. . . These are only gestures, not love itself—gestures 'which do not really seem to matter' compared with the proving of one's love in deed and in truth; and yet love lives by them. Love would die if it were not for these expressions which are not love itself at all and which *those not in love* consider superfluous 'formalities.' "[6]

Rahner's assertion is undeniable. But we might well ask ourselves about the why and wherefore of this odd—even though empirical—inversion of values. For experience after experience suggests that this moving through the "incidental" as well as the "essential" is a characteristic feature of the authenticity of the strange creature which is man in his social dimension.

Undoubtedly we must look for the secret of this characteristic in man's desperate struggle against the ambiguity of that which is "natural" in him and tends to escape his liberty more and more.[7]

Man wants to love effectively. He knows that to do this he must enter into the game of nature. He must draw out its possibilities and put them in the service of love. The only thing is that all he has at his disposal for this is his capacity to make the laws of nature work in his favor. And the same thing holds true with regard to his "second nature" acquired by education and culture.

This recourse to the natural, however provisional it may be meant to be, calls for deep immersion in natural and cultural dynamisms. They are not manipulated as an inert instrument.[8]

In group life, love cannot be efficacious without *using* persons. That is to say, it cannot be effective without reducing them to functions, even if only temporarily. This does not necessarily entail physical violence. There are other ways of using persons, such as seeing in them only the social function they represent, applying impersonal legislation to them so that they do not interfere with our concrete love, defending oneself from their claims through the use of some indirect force detached from my sensibility (e.g., a police force).[9]

What is more, a certain dimension of one's own life must be placed in the "instrumental" service of any love that seeks to be real. For example, a man knows that his love will not be efficacious if he does not bring money home. But he often senses that "bringing home the bacon" turns a large part of his life into an instrument, so that very little if anything at all remains for the initial aim and purpose: the unique intimacy of the spouses or the nuclear family.

It is here that *conscious awareness* has liberative importance. But of course it must be a *critical* consciousness, for it is a matter of getting away from a situation which is maintained, in large measure, outside of the level of consciousness. It is necessary that *suspicion* be able to arise about the whole process which has become "natural" in the twofold sense of the word. We must be able to ask certain questions. In the course of the process have I not lost the initial intention which was free and authentically social? Has it not been replaced by my submission to the law of minimum effort, by an oversimplistic synthesis, by a lumping together of individual people, by an order based on the domination of the weak by the strong—even though I be one of the weak?

But are we not caught in a vicious circle here? What can raise this suspicion but consciousness? And is it not consciousness that is alienated? Let us admit that there is something of a circle here. It is *almost* a circle, but the circle is not quite closed completely. And therein lies everything: the essence, destiny, and history of the human being and the human race.

Here appears the importance of the "incidental," the "nonessential," which may seem to be out of all proportion at first glance. Here we glimpse the importance of gesture and word or, if you prefer, of the word backed up by the gesture. It represents a minuscule quantity of energy compared to that which is invested in the "efficacious" processes of love; but by the same token this complex of gesture and word has a disproportionately large liberative influence.

1. Chesterton makes a good point about institutions in *Manalive:* even though institutions seem to be a sad affair, human beings always start to fashion them *when they are happy*. In short, they do so in the creative moments which liberty has at its disposal.[10]

It is worth noting that the gestures and words which fashion the new group well up from these creative moments. With the efficacy of an initial liberty and a happy creativity already forgotten, the first and primary function of a gesture is to *recall* the moment when love experienced the grand adventure of efficacy.

"What should be done even though love might not exist" is turned imperceptibly into "what is done even though love no longer exists." But then the gesture is suspended in mid-air, and one could say that "it is performed even though love does not exist." That is true, but it entails greater difficulty than do the things which are part and parcel of a system of efficacy. Precisely because the gesture is "incidental" and unnecessary for efficacy, precisely because it belongs almost exclusively to the plane of intentions, it is a more direct appeal to conscience. It is a call for attention from the "void" left by a mechanism which is no longer in the service of the primary intention.

2. This virtual nature of the gesture, this direct pointing at the creative finality of the group, commits the person who makes it. There is an intimate relationship *between gesture and responsibility-commitment*.

The special relationship between gesture and commitment undoubtedly lies in the same element we have just finished analyzing. Since it cannot be identified with the ambiguity of efficacy and its own proper laws, a gesture is the naked reaffirmation of an intention. Hence it questions, disturbs, and judges the person making it when the original intention, which gave rise to the gesture, is no longer present.

Paradoxically enough, man feels more twofaced in the presence of a gesture that does not express his intention than in the face of wearying activity which may have forgotten the same intention. The "incidental" is more of a summons to commitment than the essential is!

3. This dimension of commitment, which is part and parcel of the gesture, is accentuated or diluted, depending on whether the community is geared toward *responsibility* or toward a "bank-deposit" approach. In other words, when the gesture is lived in terms of *receiving*, it enters the realm of efficacy. Efficacy, be it technical or magical, envelops the gesture; and the latter thereby loses a good part of its questioning sense.

In like measure the gesture loses its unique signification every time that it is turned into a uniform mechanism just like any other mechanism. A handshake, for example, may not evoke any signification so long as I find it natural. It simply means that society accepts me. But a handshake can also express my solidarity with someone who is in trouble or anguish. It can signify a friendship renewed or recovered. The gesture is the same and yet different in such a case.

No one will confuse the formalism of offering a handshake to a guest with offering a handshake to someone who is being led off to prison. Wherein lies the difference? In the fact that in the first instance the group to which I belong is not creative or grounded on the acceptance of some responsibility. In the second case, by contrast, the gesture is not the diluted end-result of some inert group; it is the risk of forming a vital group grounded on a creative and difficult responsibility.

The latter gesture can *give me something* as well, and that may be real and important. But attention is focused on access to a group which signifies something, which feels responsible for bringing something qualitatively new into history. In this context the gesture is irreplaceable. It can never be replaced by words or theories.

Section IV

Do the sacramental signs have these characteristics? Can they have these characteristics? Here two factors would seem to condition each other. One relates to the Church, the other to the sacraments themselves.

1. As we have already indicated, no reform of the liturgy will resolve the sacramental crisis. It is not a sacramental crisis at all, but a crisis of the ecclesial community itself.

In a not too distant past which extends up to today, the order of priorities was the following. Saving grace was received in the sacraments. To be eligible for receiving them one had to act within the minimum bounds of individual conduct that were compatible with the Church. When one was disposed to go further, one had to accept the fact that the Church had an *additional* desire to play a liberative role and thereby serve the cause of mankind.

As we saw above, within such an outlook there was no way to avoid a false, "bank-deposit" conception of the sacraments. Only a Church which recognizes itself by "the name of Christ," that is, by its contribution to liberation, can give a different sense to the sacraments.

In the first place, as we saw in the last chapter, the sacraments serve as the vehicle for the responsibility of applying to historical events the basic Christian scheme of liberative interpretation: the paschal mystery. If God chose to give, along with these signs, the grace that enables the community to carry out its liberative responsibility, he did not do so because his grace has need of a rite. He did so because the community needs to be made consciously aware of the specific creativity which God gave it to inject into history.

This does not rule out the fact that the Church, a visible community, needs efficacy as all authentic love does. It too needs structures and functions, with all the ambiguity inherent in them. Hence it needs the constitutive gestures that call attention to the primary finality and responsibility.

Grace has countless signs, countless efficacious signs. But a community recognizes its unity and commitment in those signs that turn it back to its origins. It is not a morbid, paralyzing return to the past, but an exigency of creative liberty.

2. That brings us to our second question: Can the sacraments have this quality, despite the fact that all of them point to *the same* paschal happening, to *the same* reality of a love whose secret has been revealed to the Christian community? We believe that our answer to this question

can and should be affirmative. In line with that we have just seen about the function that gestures fulfill in human existence, the sacraments should be bearers of *concrete, variable, dialogic* signification—for all their apparent uniformity.

Obviously this variability can only be exemplified by taking note of the diversity in real-life situations. Let us take the baptism of children as our example here.[11] Its uniform signification is the immersion of what appears to be a merely biological life in the death of Christ. By joining with him in resurrection, this biological life makes its way to a *human* life in a community where love overcomes death. As we already noted, the question which we Christians bring to baptism is the question asked by all humanity when it is faced with the global reality of a new human being who is being incorporated into humanity. But the specific question is: Into *what* humanity is this human child being incorporated?

Here again there is a suitable general response, which is signified by a rite that is odd to people today: the rite of *exorcism*. For its new member, humanity signifies a death to the extent that it is suffused and up to a point dominated by a power, a structure, and a dynamism that is egotistical. This social—or antisocial—"demon" is exorcised by Christ's power of liberation, and conquered by his death and resurrection. Hence we must conclude that the exorcised "demon" must take on the form and signification which corresponds to the concrete threat facing this concrete human life—i.e., the life of the baptized child.

The concrete "demon" who withdraws in defeat from the existence of a child in an underdeveloped country will not be the same one who withdraws from the existence of a child in an affluent society. Nor will it be the same concrete demon for all children in the same society. One child may find a secure place wating for him, where he will be enveloped by protection and perhaps insensitivity. Another child may be threatened mainly by the possibility of being led by egotism into an existence where he is an object rather than a subject within a consumer society. Each will have his own demon.

If the sacraments are authentic gestures of the group, they must manage to express these differences and involve the community in them. We must feel the passing brush of our dominating demon, *now named and identified*. We must sense his concrete threat, now drawn out of abstact categories so that it may usher us, in spite of ourselves, into the battle in which we are concretely engaged.

Prayer which merely follows a present ritual allows the living reality to slip away. It turns the sacrament into one of those accumulative routines, which become more and more intolerable as we awaken to the liberative import of the Christian community.

Another example comes from the distant past but is still pertinent today. We find it in Paul's first letter to the Corinthians, and it concerns the Eucharist. The case is clear. It has to do with a sacrament that does more harm than good (*cf.* 1 Cor. 11:17). Why? Does it lack one of the requirements already laid down for validity? Is the presence of Christ not real in this case?

Paul's reply is surprising in terms of our present-day practice. But it must not have surprised his audience. First of all, the real situation which makes the sacrament bad instead of good is this: "When you meet as a congregation, it is impossible for you to eat the Lord's Supper, because each of you is in a hurry to eat his own, and while one goes hungry another has too much to drink" (1 Cor. 11:20). What invalidates the sacrament, then, is a situation involving the whole community rather than the dispositions of the individual. So the sacrament is in the service of the community; the latter is not there for the sake of distributing the sacraments.

But let us follow Paul. The concrete situation of the community requires that each person revise his life (*cf.* 1 Cor. 11:28). Why? Because if it is a community where some are put to shame by not possessing what others do (*cf.* 1 Cor. 11:22), then it brings judgment on itself in the service because it "does not discern the Body" (1 Cor. 11:29).

It is worth noting that this failure to discern the Lord's Body takes place in a community which knows very well that it is celebrating the Lord's Supper (*cf.* 1 Cor. 11:20,33). That is why it is responsible for the Lord's Body (*cf.* 1 Cor. 11:27,29). It recognizes it individually, we might say. But by not grasping and appreciating its import as something which calls the community into question, the community fails to discern Christ's Body. It believes it is receiving something which it is not receiving. It seeks a benefit and suffers harm.

We could just as well say that the Christian community does not discern the waters of baptism when it does not recognize its responsibility, however firmly it may believe in the efficacy of the sacrament. It does not discern penance, so long as the latter is not a questioning summons of the community and, through it, a call to liberation. And the same applies to the rest of the sacraments.

So we can sum up briefly. A community gathered together around a liberative paschal message needs signs which fashion it and question it, which imbue it with a sense of responsibility and enable it to create its own word about man's history. This is precisely what the sacraments are—and nothing else but that. Through them God grants and signifies to the Church the grace which is to constitute it truly as such within the vast human community.

NOTES TO CHAPTER FOUR

1. A repetitiveness that is formally given only in the Eucharist (much less in penance viewed in its social dimension), but which is seen even better as the repetition of the same sacraments for everybody.

2. We prefer to translate the Greek word here by "perfection." It means "end" in its positive sense of "consummation" or "fulfillment."

3. See the Pauline significance of the term "mystery" in Volume I, Appendix II (II, B, 2 and 3).

4. See CLARIFICATION I in this chapter.

5. See Volume III, Chapter IV.

6. Karl Rahner, *Theological Investigations*, II, *Man in the Church* (London: Darton, Longman and Todd; Baltimore: Helicon, 1963), pp. 129–136.

7. *Cf.* Volume II, Chapter I, main article and CLARIFICATION I.

8. Even from within a Marxist perspective, Althusser makes a keen observation about cultural dynamisms—specifically about ideologies. He notes that their power is *relatively autonomous* vis-à-vis the economic infrastructure, because they cannot be a mere *instrument* of the ruling classes. Or, to put it better, if they are to be able to be their instrument, it is necessary that those who forge them believe in them as ideology and not as instrument: "In reality the bourgeoisie has to believe in its own myth before it can convince others, and not only so as to convince others. . . . So when we speak of the class function of an ideology it must be understood that the ruling ideology is indeed the ideology of the ruling class and that the former serves the latter not only in its rule over the exploited class, *but in its own constitution of itself as the ruling class*, by making it accept the lived relation between itself and the world as real and justified" (Louis Althusser, Eng. trans., "Marxism and Humanism," in *For Marx*, New York: Pantheon Books, 1969, pp. 234–235).

9. See Volume III, Chapter IV, CLARIFICATION I.

10. See Volume II, Chapter IV, CLARIFICATION II.

11. See Chapter III, CLARIFICATION I.

CLARIFICATIONS

I. THE "BANK-DEPOSIT" APPROACH
TO EDUCATION AND SACRAMENTAL ADMINISTRATION

In a previous CLARIFICATION[1] we discussed how the distortions in the notion of efficacy parallel each other on the different planes of human existence. With what we have seen in the last two chapters, we can now try to draw an identical parallelism of a positive sort. We shall examine how to move from deformation to information, from passivity to activeness, from being an object to being a subject, from false consciousness to true consciousness-raising.

Many readers will be familiar with the relationship between this topic and the work of Paulo Freire. For he has tried to formulate and implement a pedagogy of liberation.

At the very wellsprings of Christianity, the sacraments too are a communitarian pedagogy of liberation. So we should not be surprised to find that both pedagogies, to a large extent, formulate the same criticism on the negative side and, on the positive side, are grounded on the same foundations and constructed by the same methods.

Here we shall take over statements from Paulo Frieire, simply replacing such terms as *literacy-training, education,* and *culture* with the corresponding terms in our discussion: i.e., *sacraments, grace, the Christian task,* etc.[2]

If we approach a sacrament in phenomenological terms in order to discover its essence, we will find something we have discovered earlier. There can be no true (and efficacious) sacrament if it is not a divine grace combined with its two inseparable dimensions: reflection and action. Hence the true and authentic sacrament is praxis. It is the Christian's reflection, activity, and hard work on behalf of the transformation of the world. Its business is problem-raising, never "deposit-making."

Once it sees the sacrament as this inseparable combination of reflection and action, a *critical* outlook on the process of sacramentalization rejects two things. On the one hand it rejects the alienating magic of a rite that is separated from action. On the other hand it rejects an activism in which activity is separated from reflection.

Only when it is operating from a naive outlook can our pastoral effort regard people's practical paganism (with regard to the sacraments) as a manifestation of their "lack of capacity" or "dumbness" or "laziness." A critical outlook on this same practical paganism sees it as the phenomenological explication of the parallel structure of Church and society at a given moment.

For the Church which entertains the naive view, sacramental administration is reduced to the mechanical act of "depositing" certain words, gestures, and rites in someone who is supposed to be pagan. This deposit is enough for the presumed pagan to be saved, since he thereby ceases to be a pagan.

This mechanistic conception of "ritual deposits" entails another conception that is equally naive. It is one that attributes a sense of magic to the rite. The mechanism, the rite, as a physical entity, is seen to be some sort of amulet; it is wholly independent of the person who receives it and has no relationship to the world.

From both a methodological and sociological point of view it is clear that this kind of sacramental administration, however reformed it may be, cannot be divested of its original sin. For it remains the instrument through which the grace of God is "deposited" in people. Thus the sacraments are at bottom instruments of "domestication." They almost always are alienated from people; they always alienate them. For at the very least, they rob the faithful recipient of his creative power.

So the dominant sacramental pedagogy is the pedagogy of the ruling classes. And there can be no doubt that under its false guise of sacredness this "naive" conception of sacramental administration almost always conceals its "fear of liberty." The sacraments show up, not as the preparation of people to speak their own word, but rather as a gift which the "ordained" make to the "nonordained." Thus the process of sacramental administration denies to the Christian people the possibility of uttering its own word. It is given as a gift, it is prescribed in an alienating way. And once it starts off in this way, the sacramental process cannot be an instrument for changing reality; it cannot end up affirming the recipient to be an active Christian *subject*.

A sacramental process cannot be truly Christian if it reinforces the myths with which people seek to maintain man in a dehumanized state. It can only be truly Christian if it makes an effort to inculcate a careful vigilance on reality, a vigilance wherewith the Christian turns his vocation to transform reality into an existential process. If on the other hand the process of sacramental administration emphasizes the rites and sets out to adapt man to reality, it cannot hide its dehumanizing character.

In general we can say that both the words and the rites of the sacraments have nothing to do with the existential experience of the faithful. And when they do, thanks to pastoral reforms, this relationship is drained off by being expressed in a highly paternalistic way.

That is why those who nurture a dehumanizing conception of the sacraments react against those faithful who are restless, creative, and resistant to reification. They see them as maladjusted people or rebels.

But if we do not put our confidence in the responsible Christian, who is summoned to be a subject, we succumb to manipulation and there is no longer any dialogue.

We get responsibility and commitment only when the Christian, finding himself consciously in a given "situation," asks himself about this situation and its features. Because he can emerge from it only to the extent that it ceases to be a dull and heavy weight enveloping him and pressing down on him.

Obviously no one goes through a process of consciousness-raising alone. In objectifying his world sacramentally, the faithful Christian finds himself again. But he finds himself *in* and *with* others, who are his companions in his own small circle. They find themselves and each other in the same shared world, and from the coincidence of the intentions which objectify them there arises communication. It is a dialogue that criticizes and promotes those who participate in the community. Together they critically re-create their world. What once absorbed them is now something they can see down to its depths.[3]

All this does not reduce the educator to a merely passive factor. But if he is to act and operate in the time of hsitory, he cannot do what we do when we subject man to the chronological time of the calendar. Historical time is the time of human beings, of happenings, of things to be done.

Now in the course of trying to reduce the whole significative complex to this particular time of history, the community will recognize the necessity of posing or interjecting fundamental themes relating to their situation which had not been raised before. The introduction of these themes relating to the sacraments—a proven necessity—fits in with the dialogic character of any and all education. If the communitarian setup is dialogic, then the person ordained to preside over it does have the right to participate in it with his own themes (or, those revealed by God), so long as these are not opposed to the reality through which the faithful are living.

We shall call these themes "pivotal themes." Having to do with the sacraments, they can do two things. On the one hand they may help people to comprehend a previous topic. On the other hand they can facilitate a more critical comprehension of the whole problem-complex. That is why they can come up even at the beginning of a thematic unit.

But there is a problem if the sacramental themes are not seen in their proper light—that is, in terms of their essential dimension as "borderline-limit" situations that present a challenge to man (e.g., birth and death). In that case, the tasks to which they point or the response of Christians through their activity in history may not be fulfilled in authentic, critical terms. The critical themes will be encased in the borderline-limit situations. The latter will present themselves as crushing historical determinisms which allow for nothing but adaptation or submission to them. Man will not be able to get beyond the borderline-limit situation, to glimpse or discover with the eye of faith something that stands over against the borderline-limit situation: i.e., the unexpected opening offered by divine revelation.

Thus communitarian dialogue is intersubjectivity, and it must be situated and "celebrated" as such. On the occasion of each sacrament it should present the Christian people with their present, concrete, existential situation. It should pose this situation as a problem that challenges them and calls for their response. And it should also show divine revelation to be an element capable of helping them to face up to this challenge.

The community's response, in turn, must take place on two levels: that of intellectual awareness and understanding, and that of action. When the Christian community organizes itself in sacramental terms, it orients itself toward action designed to meet an historical challenge in a reflective and critical way.

II. THE "MAN OF THE SACRAMENTS": A LIFE IN CRISIS

It is not difficult to verify the fact that there is a priestly crisis. Neither is it difficult to discard simplistic explanations and follow its track in history.

Even before Vatican II, but especially after that event, the Church defined itself as an entity in the service of humanity. But this is easier to say than to follow through to its ultimate critical consequences. And that holds true especially for those functions that are more closely related to the "ecclesiastical" realm, that is, for those which are performed in the temple and hence presided over by the priest. We cannot minimize or underestimate the fact that these functions shape our image of the priest, his place in society, and even his material sustenance.

Let us put it another way. So long as the priest's functions were seen by the faithful as something which had direct, salvific value, things that had efficacy in themselves independently of their benefit to the rest of mankind, then the priest himself felt he had a definite place in society. His functions, performed relatively well or badly and repeated without variation, were valued unreservedly by Christians. His place and station among them was recognized and indisputable, and so were his concomitant prerogatives: friendship, respect, and material support.

It would be a grave psychological and sociological error to underestimate or minimize this overall context. For at every level of society such social recognition always has a lot to do with a person's feeling of fulfillment throughout the course of his or her life. It is that which supports the person over long years of work and living, with all the problems and difficult moments entailed.

Now the fact is that this situation has changed considerably for the priest in the course of a few short years. First of all, there was Vatican II. It certainly did not denigrate the importance of the sacramental realm, of that which takes place in the domain of the temple and under the priest's control. But it did relativize all this in a positive sense, by tying in its value with the service of the Christian community to the human community in general.

Secondly, we cannot get away from the issue by simply saying it means that the priest has the possibility and the duty of contributing to man's liberation at every level. That is an escapist presentation which hides a critical and gnawing problem. The fact is that the classic, age-old tasks of the Church are being judged by those most committed to social reform in terms of their relationship with sociopolitical needs; and the latter have become extremely critical and urgent, at least in under-developed countries. Since the Medellín Conference spoke out boldly and forthrightly against a sitution of "internal and external colonialism," this very situation has produced a rapid process of radicalization among people in the countries of Latin America which were considered to be the most stable. Within a span of five years or less, these countries are now faced with unforeseen and intolerable options.

What was once seen as a matter of tying in certain ecclesial tasks with service to the community has now become something else for many Christians. For them it is now a matter of minimizing or judging as irrelevant those ecclesial tasks which seem to be nontemporal, self-contained, repetitive, impervious to outside happenings and hence inca-pable of having a decisive influence on them. And to this realm of tasks belong those which in the past have been attributed invariably to the priest—the sacramental realm, to begin with.

Here we have the two elements which have now converged to fashion the present-day crisis in the priestly ministry. Let us take a look at each in turn.

1. We will begin with the second. As everybody knows, the structures and the poverty of a large part of the Latin American continent may not have changed very much in the last few years, but there has been much change in the critical awareness of many sectors. This has brought a great deal of change in their demands and their activities. Included in these factions would be populist politicians, labor unionists, student organizations, a fair portion of the middle class, and guerrilla movements in cities and the countryside. The shift is embodied in the coming to power of socialist or socialist-leaning regimes in various countries.

In the face of these events, there has been an increase in general aggressiveness and in the urgency of both factions to find and implement measures and to work up pronouncements and position papers. Long-run solutions are systematically shunted aside. Conservative governments defend themselves from criticism by engaging in repression. The repres-sed sectors in turn—and particularly young people—see the immediate modification of structures as the only way out; and they do not hestitate to sacrifice future possibilities since the latter seem to be too distant and quite impossible of realization.

Most of the visible functions of the Church are framed within this generalized atmosphere of aggressiveness and urgency. The situation is all the more critical because the potential efficacy of these functions is seen to be very long-term or even completely atemporal. In this set of circumstances the presence of the priest is disputed by two forces which, for all their opposition to each other, combine to contribute to the priest's own crisis.

Some persons, groups, and classes desperately and aggressively seek to maintain the present situation in its general outlines. As everyone knows, they are rediscovering the "nontemporal" aspect of the Church—and more specifically, the traditional tasks of the priest. They see this aspect as one of the last agents of social stability, and they are clinging to it. This stance generates an attitude toward the priest which differs markedly from the one entertained years ago, even though appreciation of his functions is one of its hallmarks. For it is marked by a suspicious "big brother" outlook rather than by one of respect. It is paternalistic, and tends to turn the priest into a mere tool.

On the opposite front, some persons and groups are driven relentlessly by the chance to put through structural reforms. They see this chance within their grasp. They have less and less appreciation for the nontemporal features of priestly tasks, for their remote efficacy, and for a repetitiveness which is almost completely devoid of reference to what these people regard as the one and only burning question and the one and only decisive option. At best the priest may say something in a Sunday sermon or contribute his presence to a discussion meeting.

Hence the priest does not feel he is appreciated by the very people with whom he may well agree. And if he is, the appreciation carries an implied criticism of the vague and remote nature of his function. They would appreciate him more as a leader—if he has the necessary qualifications of course—and they bewail everything about his place in time, his style of life (e.g., celibacy), and his work, all of which separate him from urgent sociopolitical tasks. Added to that is the fact that even this positive valuation of him makes him feel a sense of responsibility, giving rise to feelings of impatience and frustration with regard to conservative or neutral ecclesiastical attitudes, including those beyond his control.

Between these two critical polarizations, which are difficult to support or tolerate in the long run, the traditional "average Catholic" seems to have disappeared. We no longer seem to have the faithful member who relates spontaneously to the priest as such and to his real-life activity and feelings. And while one may claim that all this seems relatively theoretical, one would be greatly mistaken to minimize its impact on priestly life over the course of months and years.

2. Before we go on to spell out more about the crisis in priestly life resulting from sociopolitical radicalization, we must analyze the impact of its other source: namely, the opening of the Church to secular problems and, particularly in Latin America, to the burning issues posed by the cause of human liberation.

The Church adopted this position publicly and officially at Vatican II. It was especially evident in *Gaudium et spes*. And it was applied even more concretely to the context of Latin America in the statements issued by the Medellín Conference—particularly in its major documents on justice and peace.

But with this step, signalized in the famous opening statement of *Gaudium et spes,* the Church has entered into a process that is often repeated in history. At the moment a statement is made, people see only its liberative content; they do not yet see its difficult implications or the critical consequences that logically flow from it.

Supposedly we are to introduce the joys and hopes and sorrows and anxieties of Latin Americans into the very being and central activity of the Church—not just into her incidental, reflex activity. Supposedly the liberation of Latin American man from *all* his enslavements is a central and essential task of the Church and her salvific mission. But if all this is true, it will inevitably call the accustomed structure of the Church into serious question. If we plant such an explosive change, then the Church cannot continue plodding along to eternity by carrying out her customary tasks.

In any case it has called into question the accustomed function of the priest. Such a result was not contemplated perhaps, but it was inevitable. And the impact is all the more forceful in that it was not foreseen, because it did not allow the priest to prepare for what was coming.

First of all, the priest's functions have been traditionally reduced to liberation from individual sinfulness exclusively, and an *unseen* liberation at that. This was the ultimate aim of confession, baptism, anonymous Communion, preaching, and last rites. And it was this same attitude that fashioned the primary real-life cell of the Church: *the parish.* On a secondary level, it also gave rise to the Catholic school, which was incapable of posing the problem of liberation in another context because of its ideological and class homogeneity.

It would be a delusion to pretend that *liberation of the individual from sin,*[4] expanded in scale, could bring about all the other needed liberations in an effective, rapid, or even realistic way; that there is no need to call into question the sinful[5] sociopolitical structures which are responsible for the most tangible and urgent enslavements: poverty, hunger, ignorance, exploitation, etc. These can only be overcome by an attack on structures. That is to say, the attack must be directed at the source from which they come.

So the problem is that the Church could not possibly continue to carry on its activity centered around the territorial parish without accentuating the crisis in the priestly ministry. That is a logical consequence of the new orientation laid down by Vatican II, however unforeseen it may have been.

Up to now the parish has been the most faithful embodiment of a Church in which the *means* was minimal membership in the community and the *end* was reception of the sacraments that ensured salvation to all. But throughout this book we have seen that there is a clear orientation in the opposite direction, which runs from the gospel to Vatican II. It says that the sacraments are *means* to form and set in motion an ecclesial community, since its liberative influence constitutes its true *end*.

It is not easy to opt pastorally for the latter alternative, especially on the institutional level. But if we accept the conciliar orientations and their implications and then continue to keep the priest at his old functions and activities, we cannot avoid heightening this crisis more in the upcoming years—even though the simple routine of parochial activities may seem to extenuate it for the time being. And even when we grant the influence of the last-mentioned factor, we would do well to note how the lack of consistency between the conciliar image of the priest and his real-life duties is converging in the problem of vocations.

Secondly, let us suppose that the classic priestly duties—be they parochial or not—should continue to remain in force without being called into question. From a psychological and sociological point of view, one thing is obvious in a context of urgency and crisis such as that which pervades Latin America. These tasks can no longer bring fulfillment to a man's whole life if they are not integrated with a specific contribution to human liberation.

The point here is that the establishment of a close relationship between priestly functions and the whole secular realm of man's sociopolitical problems is not as easy as one might think. And the difficulty is not due solely to the urgency now attributed to these problems. Nor does it depend exclusively on whether one adopts a preconciliar or postconciliar posture. Even the basic practical difficulties are appreciable.

However much it may have been revised, the theological formation of the priest remains at bottom what it was before Vatican II and the Medellín Conference. There is now more stress on some topics than on others, to be sure, and the contributions of more modern authors are taken into account. But its two dominant characteristics remain the same. 1. Theology is handed out *readymade and complete* to be learned and retained. The assumption is that later on, in one's priestly practice, what has been learned passively will magically enable one to relate the Christian message to the unforeseen and confusing events he will have to live through. 2. *Moral* theology, which will later inspire one's liberative praxis and say what should be done in the face of real-life happenings, is totally separated from dogma in its methodology. It is boxed in a series of formulas, while dogma is related to orthodoxy.

To put it in other words, we might use the training of a medical doctor as an example. He is taught to diagnose the illness of a patient in an active way. Without this all his theoretical training would remain highly uncertain. The seminarian, by contrast, is taught certain practical procedures that are equivalent to the training of a nurse. He is left in the dark about the concrete way of interpreting the signs of the times in the light of the Christian message.

So we see a growing uncertainty and insecurity in the seminarian as he looks toward the priesthood. And we see an even more dramatic option being posed in the life of the priest. One alternative for him is to remain a stranger to the problems of time and history, limiting his remarks and decisions to the things he was taught once and for all in the seminary. The other alternative is for him to interpret real-life happenings like any other kid on the corner or man in the street, blurting out what he sees in his own foggy way and then perhaps adding some hasty justification from the gospel that is highly questionable. And this justification may be rejected for some good reason by some and judged superfluous by others.

There is another important point here for which the liberative declarations of Vatican II and Medellín did not make adequate provision. They did not take due account of their impact on the life and task of the priest.

Suppose it is true that the function of liberating mankind is an important and decisive part of the Church's mission. Suppose that the priest's work should be aimed in that direction—not directly, but through his work of raising the consciousness of the community with the help of divine revelation. If all that is true, we cannot minimize the impact it will have on the very sustenance of the priest.

It is obvious that provisions have not been made for different means of livelihood that would fit in with this relatively new function demanded of the priest. In most places and for the most part, he continues to depend for his livelihood on those things which seem to be invariable and to have no relationship with liberation and its problems. The work that he might be able to do with respect to preparing the Christian community for this task is not a major or even adequate source of a basic living budget. Any important modification in the present setup—not to mention the replacement of the present parochial structure—would leave him without means of support in many places. If such modification is not forthcoming, on the other hand, the priest must face a wearisome and crushing time in which there is no room for study and reflection. And while he may have been able to prescind from these things once upon a time, he cannot now as he seeks to reformulate his role and task. Is this not often the source of the crisis of esteem which he faces from the faithful, and in particular from study groups which could be the seeds of real base communities?

Added to this is the fact that giving the role of the priest a liberative cast not only does not help his means of support and sustenance; it also generates ecclesiastical conflicts in many cases, quite aside from the civil conflicts mentioned earlier.

The first and primary cause of these ecclesiastical conflicts has already been alluded to. The liberative cast attributed to the priest's task is often not accompanied by a corresponding response within the priest. That is, he does not engage in a serious effort to interpret the Christian message or historical reality. He is not prepared for such an effort. Willy-nilly

he absorbs criteria and urgencies that are supported by certain political
or social groups, whether they be correct or not. In such cases he jeopar-
dizes the capacity of the Christian community to transcend the limited
nature of the present moment or of a given concrete solution (GS 43)
by reading and interpreting its own message in a broader, deeper, and
ultimately more liberative context. In other words, commitment is
required of the Church; but in ecclesial terms it may be immature,
narrow, superficial.

The second cause of ecclesiastical conflicts is also relatively simple
and clearcut. Even when it is well done, this required transformation
of the priestly task in critical sociopolitical situations generates difficulties
for the hierarchy. It in turn reacts negatively in the face of objections
raised by lay groups and civil authorities who are interested in maintaining the status quo and using the Church to this end. In such cases
one often hears threats of legislative changes which could affect the
Church in some way, particularly in terms of its influence on the level
of the masses. Here again the optimism of hierarchical declarations,
such as those of Medellín, fails to show up *in situ.*

The third cause of ecclesiastical conflicts is more complicated. On
the practical level, the aforementioned transformation of the priestly
task does not take place in a uniform manner anywhere. Even so-called
"joint pastoral efforts" allow for abysmal differences at this level. As
a result, the priest does not feel he is backed up by his corps of colleagues.
There are many priests who find it easier to relate to other Christians
and even atheists than to most of their colleagues in the priesthood.
Awake to this fact, lay people often do not trust the priest as the authentic
representative of the Church. They attribute what he does to his
psychological makeup, his ideological bent, or his political stance. After
all, the next parish does just the opposite!

What we have said in this section should indicate the range of the
problems that meet in the present crisis of the sacerdotal ministry. It
would be sad indeed if this crisis were not viewed and analyzed in terms
of this overall context. But that is precisely what happens when surveys
deal only with the consequences of the crisis (mental prayer, spiritual
direction, praying the breviary) and not with its causes (which are often
unconscious). That is also what happens when stress is placed on factors
that are certain (such as celibacy), but that only acquire force within
a crisis of a much more total nature. Finally, that is what happens when
we offer simplistic solutions: manual labor, family life, implementation
of the diaconate.

Here again we must repeat what we have said before. It is not a crisis
in the priesthood. It is a crisis in the internal coherence of the Church.

III. THE TRANSITION FROM MAGIC TO SIGN

It should be clear from the previous CLARIFICATIONS that the ecclesial
transformation which stirs up the greatest resistance is the most concrete

one. It could not be otherwise. Just as in civil society, it is when reforms touch upon the critical, sensitive points that the option shows up in all its clarity. Either we turn back, still talking about "reform," or else reform turns into a revolution. In the life of the Church, it is when reforms touch upon the concrete tasks which absorb most of the time of her ecclesiastical personnel that she must make a decision about options which seemed very acceptable and progressive in theory: i.e., the Church as a community of service; salvation as liberation.

Hence the critical point of any pastoral effort is not whether sacramental life is going to be reformed. All are agreed on that, whether they like it or not. But the decisive point is whether this reform will be put through *gradually* or not. Will it be implemented at a prudent pace which will follow the rhythm of the masses and not risk everything at once? And if it is done in that way, can we really shift from a magical type of sacramental system to the consciousness-raising sacramental system, intimately related to faith and history, that Vatican II wanted?

We can sum up the issue in a series of questions. Is it possible to shift *gradually* from one to the other? Or must we have a qualitative change, starting from the other end and discarding what has been built up with so much effort?

This is what accounts for the anxiety that gnaws at many pastors—in secret or out in the open. This is what accounts for the impatience of many of the faithful with what seems to be an incomprehensible hesitation. This is what accounts for the fact that if we do not manage to give a just response to this question, we end up by resorting to the expedient of juxtaposing two opposing pastoral efforts and pretending that they are complementary. And we label them in such a way that no one dare choose between them: e.g., pastoral care of *the masses*— pastoral care for *the elites*.

But since the fundamental question still continues to be a reasonable one, indeed the only reasonable one, we must at least discuss the problem. Without pretending to offer a satisfactory solution, we shall try to indicate some of the points that stand out clearly from what we have already said.

1. Sacrament *qua* sacred rite and sacrament *qua* sign of ecclesial responsibility do not constitute two levels or grades of one and the same motivation—one corresponding to "elites," the other to the "masses" or the "people." A magical conception of the sacraments has undeniably been evident in the Church (GS 7). But it and the authentic evangelical conception of the sacraments, as we have already pointed out,[6] spring from motives that are not only different but opposed to each other. One is motivated by security and it turns membership in the Church into its instrument. The other is motivated by a sense of communitarian responsibility and it turns the signs into its instruments.

These different motivations, along with their corresponding value-scales, have no serious tie-in with the sociological designations: "elite" and "masses." It is not through class, education, or wealth[7] that one overcomes insecurity and directs one's life toward personal responsibility. What is more, if the current sacramental system is a pacifying ideological element which helps to maintain the present status quo of society, then it is from the people that the new understanding of the sacramental realm can come. It will not come from the elites who are involved in and committed to this status. Experience alone proves that.

2. This is not to suggest that the majority of society as a whole is inclined to move from sacraments which guarantee security—here or in the hereafter—to sacraments that will necessarily commit it to a critical process aimed at liberating us from all the bondages that weigh upon mankind.

Thus the difficulty shifts from being a sociological problem to a problem of value-scales. If we conceive the sacraments as something worthwhile no matter what the motivation behind them is,[8] then it is only logical to prefer that they be sacraments of "the people" or of "the masses" even though they are an opiate, rather than that they be the sacraments of minority groups even though the latter may be liberators of the people.

This should not be regarded as an offensive way of posing the problem. If someone is convinced that a particular thing has value for its own sake, and indeed eternal value, then it is only logical for him to want to make it available to the greatest possible number of people and to disregard the course that leads to that end. Only when the course itself is included in the valuation process, indeed only when it becomes the dominant factor in the evaluation, does the problem of motivation begin to take on more importance than the number of people that the thing reaches. And this is not due to any elitist conception. It is due to the plain and simple fact that the masses will change only after the minority groups have shouldered a sense of responsibility toward them rather than serenely participating in their continued domination.

3. But we have still to tackle the most practical aspect of our task: How can we move in a positive way to effect the transition from one conception to the other, from one motivation to the other?

First of all we must admit that the existing religiosity, which is magical rather than critical, operates mainly as one of the many elements of our culture and in interaction with the rest. So we cannot indulge in the fantasy that we can have the partial evolution of something which is intimately bound up with other cultural elements that are still more powerful. Such partial evolution is not possible precisely because the general religious element is not critical toward the totality of which it forms a part. Only after the Christian conscience has acquired this critical attitude will it be able to acquire a greater measure of independence vis-a-vis the other elements of our culture.

Religiosity will not be radically altered, nor will Christians be brought from one motivation to its opposite, through some unconscious process or through religious instruments that remain submerged in the overall culture.

The transition from motives based on personal security to motives based on personal responsibility will normally take place on the more concrete and demanding plane of civic life and its urgent problems.[9] And from there people will shift to a parallel motivation in the life of the Church.[10]

This does not mean that pastoral work has nothing to do in the interim. Right now one of the key points of our pastoral effort is the work of establishing and facilitating contacts between the Church and those people who are living through this process of transforming their motives in the face of urgent sociopolitical questions. These contacts must be regarded as decisive, even though the people involved may not be in close touch with sacramental life at present. To put it mildly, the present-day structure of the Church does not foster such contacts.

We regard this as a key point because one of the most evident signs of reform in ecclesial life at present consists in establishing quite a different sort of contact. It is the various contacts that arise from people's demands for the sacraments. Quite apart from the time and personnel and resources this entails, the fact is that this sort of "religious" contact is not the answer. Such sporadic contact, totally divorced from the problems which can create a sense of responsibility, cannot link the Church with true and sound sacramental motivations—to which an impressive number of people might be disposed by some other approach.

4. By the same token we should not underestimate the potential for change in the masses that frequent the Church. But there is a condition attached. We must not be afraid of the consequences of a pastoral effort that is clearly aimed at instilling a new motivation. In other words, we cannot present this new pastoral effort as complementary to the other or geared toward it.

We must start off by accepting the fact that the Christian people in general do not possess the correct conception of the Church and its functions. Why? Because they have not received Christianity as the "good news" about the mystery of death and resurrection.

This presupposes certain things about our pastoral effort, and about our preaching in particular. Instead of dwelling on the *consequences* of something which the people do not in fact possess yet, it must take sufficient time to dwell upon the essential reality of the gospel and the function of the Church. It must not be afraid to repeat the fundamental points over and over again, to resist the temptation of rushing through to the last page. This sober, insistent, creative preaching may repel many. But in as many others it will establish a relationship with their own transformation and consciousness-raising in other areas of life. From there will come the new motivation capable of transforming them into a real community and an authentic sacramental Church.

NOTES

1. Chapter II, CLARIFICATION I.

2. The whole text of this section, except for the substitutions indicated above, is taken from the contribution of Paulo Freire to our joint effort, *Contribución al Proceso de Concientización en América Latina,* supplement to the periodical *Cristianismo y Sociedad,* Montevideo, 1968.

3. This paragraph, by way of exception, is taken from the contribution of Hernani M. Fiori to the aforementioned effort.

4. *Cf.* Volume II, Chapter I, CLARIFICATION III.

5. *Cf.* Thus in the Medellín documents there is one on pastoral care of the masses and a separate one on pastoral concern for the elites. See MED II, 119–126; 127–136. The bishops of Argentina met in San Miguel (April 21–26, 1969) to consider how to adapt the conclusions of Medellín to their nation. Their document (*Declaración del Episcopado Argentino*) chooses to speak of pastoral care for the people (*pastoral popular*) rather than pastoral care of the masses (*pastoral de masas*).

8. "No matter what the motivation behind them is" does not mean prescinding from the minimal moral and legal prerequisites for receiving the sacraments. These continue in force, but without attacking the problem as to why people have recourse to the sacraments.

9. Even here John's observation is valid: "But if a man says, 'I love God', while hating his brother, he is a liar. If he does not love the brother whom he has seen, it cannot be that he loves God whom he has not seen" (1 John 4:20). Priority in the wellsprings of love arises from life in its most simple and least ideologized form. It is there that one accepts or rejects the responsibility that fits him for the Church.

10. Experiences in Latin American countries have shown, for example, that when simple people are introduced to the real life of labor unionism and its intensified stress on struggle and responsibility, the first reaction is one of withdrawal from their previous (magical) religiosity. Only after taking this step and facing this crisis do they begin to understand and appreciate the real motivating force behind authentic Christian community.

Conclusion

Starting with the first chapter of this book, or more accurately, from the very wellsprings of faith, we saw an opposition arise to full expression and then move toward its ultimate consequences. It was an opposition between rite and sign, and we have seen the Christian option in favor of the latter.

Obviously it is not terminology that interests us here. From an historical point of view, for example, it would not be difficult to prove that the word "rite" can have a positive sense.

What does interest us here is the opposition between two different conceptions of the sacramental realm. And the vocabulary used simply seemed apt for expressing it and for summoning the reader to a real rather than a merely verbal option.

Our feeling and hope is that now, at the end of this book, the reader can see clearly the profound difference in focus of interest that is represented by "rite" and "sign" as ways of understanding the sacraments in the life of the Church.

We live in a world where every day sees a sharpening in the conflicts that envelop the great masses of mankind. One need only consider that malnutrition kills more than thirty million human beings each year—almost as many casualties as in World War II. One need only realize that an irrepressible urgency for liberation has sprouted over the past few years in the so-called Third World: i.e., the exploited periphery of the great economic empires. In this context the most important fact, which obligates theology to study both it and itself, is the growing participation of Christians in the movement for liberation—or, at the very least, the uneasy conscience spawned by the participation of Christians in the vanguard of this movement.

The official stances of the ecclesiastical hierarchy in Latin America have not remained fixed in neutrality. Some people criticize the analyses in the Medellín documents for being deficient, for being more descriptive than profound and dialectical. But no one, least of all the conservative and reactionary sectors of the Church, have failed to grasp its most significant decisions. Even on this hierarchical level, where the conflicts faced by the laity every day in their societal and political life are dampened down, we can see a change not only in tone but also, and especially, in preoccupations.

When we compare the documents of Medellín with those of Vatican II, which came earlier, we note an obvious shift of attention from intramural ecclesiastical problems to those posed by the necessity of relating the essence of the Christian message with the task of liberating man.[1] And this fact cannot help but have a profound effect on all the basic notions of our faith—not for the sake of trading them in for others but for the sake of giving them the ring of truth that only commitment to history can give them. Certainly the way we comprehend the liturgy and the sacraments is one of these *basic* notions.[2]

It is obvious that this difference or even opposition in focus of interest can be turned into a radical one, so that we end up at extremist, one-sided positions where the church-world dialectic is eliminated. By situating our preference in the notion of *sign* (on the basis of the gospel itself), we seek to do two things. Firstly, we want to preserve the necessary and difficult tension of the church-world dialectic. Secondly, we want to forestall simplistic attempts to reform the liturgy and the sacramental awareness of the faithful, attempts which turn their back on the process of history.

Preserving the tension mentioned above means understanding and accepting the fact that the transformations which must be introduced into the world and the reforms that must be put through in the Church condition each other reciprocally.

This implies two important things. First of all it means that the Church and its structures do not stand over against the world but rather are within the world. Hence it is false to assume that it is possible to put through intra-ecclesial reform first so that we may then serve the world better. For the fact is that this very service must enter into the picture as a criterion of that reform.

This whole book has tried to show that the tendency to reform the Church from within falls into a ritualistic dualism that is opposed to the gospel. This is particularly true in the extreme forms that disavow any political involvement, whether they go by the name of supernaturalism, or eschatology, or whatever. The danger is far from being remote. For all the talk about service to the world, this "world" is seen as an external reality. And the feeling is that it will undoubtedly benefit on the rebound from any improvement in the inner structures or mentality of Christianity, however much the latter may be geared toward religious finality.

Thus one part of the Church uses a new vocabulary but continues to be a basically static reality, turning its back on the one, divine historical vocation of man.

In the volumes of this series we have been touching upon the tangible points where the Church of Christ plays out its destiny. But with this theme, perhaps more than with any other, we come to a concrete decision; and it is to be noted that it is a typically ecclesiastical theme. Looking at the sacraments, we must decide whether the *raison d'être* of the Church does or does not reside *in the Church itself*. In other words, the question is whether her internal structure and her normal intramural functioning constitute the normal point of reference when we are trying to give the Church her quality of service through her process of historical evolution.[3]

Faced with this choice, we fully realize that superficial references to the texts of Vatican II will not suffice.[4] The fact is that the Constitution on the Liturgy, *Sacrosanctum Concilium,* was the first document promulgated by that assembly. It had the great merit of breaking with the juridical ritualism that had been backed up by the habitual or accustomed conduct of the Church. But one cannot deny that it is still focused primarily on the Church's intramural life—as if that reality were capable of deciding what was authentic liturgical worship without confronting the world.

Thus, at the Council, the liturgy did not undergo the same corrective process that ecclesiology did, for example. It did not move from an intramural, isolated conception of itself to a confrontation between its own essence and the exigencies of the present-day world. It did not move from *Lumen gentium* to *Gaudium et spes.* It would be a naive betrayal of the Council to think that the two latter Constitutions say *the same thing* about the Church. It would be just as naive to think that *Sacrosanctum Concilium* need not have gone through a similar confrontation.

The second important point is this. Preserving the church-world tension also means refusing to replace the sacramental realm with an historical efficacy derived from a process of analysis in which divine revelation does not have a concrete communitarian influence.

The fact is that there is a tension at work here. On the one hand, historical conflicts grow sharper and come to a head. On the other hand, we seek to educate the Christian community so that, enlightened in part by this history (i.e., by the signs of the times), it may contribute the message of revelation to this same concrete history. Neither revelation without history, nor history without revelation: we must have both. For we know that only their mutual interaction can bear fruitful results. And this interaction must affect both right from the start.

This is the challenge that confronts the whole Christian community. Only by accepting this challenge will it rediscover the sacraments.

NOTES TO CONCLUSION

1. In the world today there are more than three hundred periodicals specializing in theology, biblical studies, liturgy, and pastoral problems. To get an idea of how novel is this change in preoccupations, which stems from the need Christians feel for a tieup between their faith and their commitment to man's liberation, one need only check to see how little evident this tieup is in the vast panorama of theological literature. A young Christian reading these periodicals would be struck dumb by their lack of social sensitivity and their naive failure to appreciate the influence exerted by sociopolitical situations on theological themes.

2. Therefore it is not odd to find that in Latin America the dividing line between conservatives and progressives does not coincide with the distinction between "preconciliar" and "postconciliar" attitudes. There are outlooks which can legitimately be called postconciliar, but which in fact get nothing out of the Council but a simple reform. They overlook the profound change of mentality which this seems to presuppose as far as the Council is concerned—at least as it is read by others such as the bishops gathered at Medellín.

3. The recognition of universal history and its needs as one pole of reference for the whole Church, and not simply one more area among its preoccupations, is perhaps one of the reasons why Latin America—even more than Europe's nascent "political theology," has its own original witness to present to the rest of the Church.

4. For this reason the conciliar texts will not simply be presented in this volume, as they were in the preceding ones of this series. Here they will be examined in terms of their inner consistency and logic. See Appendix II.

Appendices

Appendices

APPENDIX I

Introduction to the Series

FORMAT AND ORIGIN OF THIS SERIES

We have tried to make it easier for the reader to approach this series by using a coherent format. The essential aspects of our reflection on a given topic are contained in the initial article under each chapter. They are followed by a section entitled CLARIFICATIONS, in which we try to develop and apply more concretely the central lines of thought, to suggest study topics and related issues, and to go over one or more points in detail. Notes are given at the end of each of these two main divisions.

The notes are meant to be useful to the reader rather than to be erudite. Many of them are biblical, indicating other passages in Scripture which complement the thoughts presented or which can be used for related meditation. Instead of citing numerous scholarly works, we have limited ourselves to a few more accessible sources: e.g., the *Concilium* series. Our series was originally intended for a Latin American audience, and their needs were uppermost in our minds.

The type of theological reflection presented here can give rise to different discussion formats: full-length courses, study weeks, and the like. But we actually tested it in a seminar approach, involving intensive sessions of study, discussion, and prayer. It may interest the reader to know how our seminars actually operate.

As far as length of time is concerned, our experiences confirmed the feeling that the busy layman benefits more from short-term seminars in which he is actively involved than from long-term courses in which he is generally passive. So now we try to run seminars of three or four days that coincide with a holiday weekend. The aim is to provide five or six sessions of four hours each in a relatively short space of time. We also stress that enrollment in the seminar implies that the individual is willing to involve himself in it totally, to participate in all the sessions, and to remain until it is over. The seminar is meant to be a total experience, not mere attendance at a series of lectures.

Each four-hour session operates pretty much like this. It begins with a lecture (which is reproduced almost verbatim as the initial section of each chapter). The lecture lasts about one hour, and at its conclusion one or two questions are proposed to the various study groups (see Appendix IV in this volume). But before they move into their discussion groups, the participants are asked to spend a few moments in personal meditation on the questions. In this way they can make an effort to formulate a personal solution, however provisional it might be, to the questions posed.

The various study groups then spend about forty-five minutes to an hour in discussing the questions. There are no more than ten persons in a given group, so that each individual will participate actively in the discussion. Herein lies the essential aim of the seminar itself, for the participants are supposed to move on from formulated truths to a truly interiorized truth. In other words, the discussion represents a confrontation between what they have heard and what they have learned from their real-life experiences; between that which they accepted uncritically as children and adolescents and that which they have put together into a coherent whole as adults.

Thus the questions proposed are not meant to serve as a review of the lecture material. They are meant to foster a greater coherence between that which was provided in the lecture and other aspects or facts of Christian experience. To this end, it is highly desirable that the groups be somewhat heterogeneous in makeup, and that their discussion be stimulated by a pointed confrontation with things they may have read in the catechism or heard all their life from the pulpit.

It is also highly useful at this point to have the groups make an effort to reach unanimity on their answers and to write them up as a group project. Such a procedure obliges the participants to engage in a real dialogue and to respect differences of opinion. When this period is over, the various groups reassemble at a roundtable forum, and each group presents the answers it has formulated. The reply of the group may take one of three forms: a unanimous group response, a set of differing opinions, or a series of questions formulated by the group. It is our feeling that questions worked up by a group are more useful than those which an individual might formulate alone at the end of the lecture.

During the roundtable forum, the lecturer comments on the group replies, tries to respond to the questions of the various groups, and then takes up individual questions if he so desires.

The procedure varies for the final hour. Intellectual effort gives way to a period of prayer and recollection that is related to the theme under consideration. It may involve some form of paraliturgical service, or a biblical reading that is not discussed in great detail (see Appendix III in this volume).

This pattern is repeated throughout the course of the seminar. As circumstances permit, the final four-hour session may be dedicated to a review of what has been covered and a discussion of possible concrete applications in the local or parochial sector.

As the reader will see from the text itself, our aim is not to move on to a wholly different topic in each four-hour session. Experience has shown that it is more useful to return to the same few basic ideas over and over again, relating them ever more deeply to real-life problems. It is useful, in this connection, to sum up what has gone before at the start of each session. One practical way of doing this is to refer to conciliar texts that relate to the material in question (see Appendix II in this volume). While we do not feel that these texts by themselves are enough to encourage this type of reflection, we do find that they are able to shore up and confirm the work already done. For they come from the universal Church gathered together in our day under the special action of the Holy Spirit.

Finally we would point out that this treatment of the sacraments has been preceded by a volume on the Church (Volume I), a volume on grace (Volume II), and a volume on God (Volume III), and that it will be followed by a volume on sin and redemption (Volume V). Each year a seminar is held on a new topic, and seminars on old topics are held for those who have not yet attended them. In this way we hope to answer the needs of mature persons who are looking for a theology which is equally adult, which is open to exploring new pathways related to their temporal commitments.

APPENDIX II

Pertinent Conciliar Texts

Vatican II introduced something unforeseen into the corpus of a Church which, for all practical purposes, is divided into parishes: i.e., into territorial units divided up for the purposes of sacramental administration.[1] And it introduced this element, not specifically when it was talking about the sacraments, but rather when it brought the problems of the world closer to the very center of the Church's life and final goal.

Thus it is not surprising that the different "postconciliar" attitudes are logically regarded in terms of this *criterion of proximity* or nearness. If one is to be consistent, then his concrete way of understanding the sacraments will depend on this sort of criterion. And one might well add this: since the Church is in practice organized around the sacramental realm, it is there that the different theoretical conceptions and their practical consequences will be most clearly visible.

Now all the preceding remarks in this book can and should be viewed as the logical development of *one* of the interpretations that are presently being given to a certain conciliar passage. This passage, which deals specifically with the position of the problems of history in relation to the very heart of the Church's task, is particularly difficult. It comes from *Gaudium et spes,* the high point of the Council's theological reflection. This is what it says:

> Earthly progress must be carefully distinghished from the growth of Christ's kingdom. Nevertheless, to the extent that the former can contribute to the better ordering of human society, it is of vital concern to the kingdom of God (GS 39).

How are we to interpret this passage, which is more important for the theology and pastoral practice of the sacraments than the whole conciliar Constitution on the Liturgy? Well, anyone who does make the careful distinction suggested in this passage cannot help but situate sacramental activity in the realm of the kingdom and its growth. So that forces one to ask himself what is the correct relationship between the sacraments and earthly progress.

It is our feeling that there are three possible interpretations here, each endowed with a certain logic, supported by certain conciliar texts, and entailing very definite and specific options. The third interpretation is the one that we have opted for in this volume.

I Two Histories and Two Efficacies

The first interpretation is that the finality of temporal progress and the finality of the kingdom and its growth are *really different*—even though both are willed by God. One is *natural* (that of earthly progress), the other is *supernatural* (that of the kingdom and its growth). In the realm of the visible, moreover, one is *profane* and the other is *religious*. Each has its own *means*, and the efficacy of the sacraments *ex opere operato* obviously is to be included among the religious means; for it is situated and operative only within the order of religious, supernatural finality.

A. CONCILIAR SUPPORT

There is certainly no lack of conciliar texts that fit in with the classic conception, prevalent at least since Trent, and give support to this interpretation.

For example, we find conciliar passages that speak about the efficacy of the Church in history (i.e., on temporal progress) as a *reflection* of its *specific and distinctive* activity on behalf of salvation—the latter activity being exercised on a different plane (i.e., that of the kingdom and its growth).

> Pursuing the saving purpose which is proper to her, the Church not only communicates divine life to men, but in some way casts the *reflected light* of that life over the entire earth (GS 40).

What is more, not only is the finality of the Church distinghished from earthly progress; it is also defined as salvific without having any intrinsic relationship with earthly progress.

> The Church, now sojourning on earth as an exile, is necessary for salvation. For Christ, made present to us in His body, which is the Church, is the one Mediator and the unique Way of salvation. In explicit terms He Himself affirmed the necessity of faith and baptism. . . and thereby affirmed also the necessity of the Church, for through baptism as through a door men enter the Church (LG 14).

As the reader can see, it is not just that two ends are distinguished from one another. In fact the second one is relativized, if only by omission. It is made subordinate to the one which is qualified as decisive by the very choice of words—*salvation*, etc. And it is also evident that this decisive attribute applies to the sacraments, which are the means to this salvific finality and end.

It is interesting to note that this interpretation, for all that, does take in and assimilate one idea that was greatly stressed by the Council: i.e., that the Church is or should be at the service of the rest of mankind.

Following logically from the preceding framework, the first service the Church can perform is that of conquest—even though that term is not used. In other words, the Church can operate to see to it that the majority of mankind reach that minimum level where the specific and distinctive means of salvation can operate on them. This would mean the sacraments which, as we have seen, are defined without any relation to earthly progress. This is how Christians, insofar as they are Christians, ought to act in the world—seeing that the distinction between final ends logically leads to a distinction between two types of duties:

> Because the very plan of salvation requires it, the faithful should learn how to distinguish carefully between those rights and duties which are theirs as members of the Church, and those which they have as members of human society. Let them strive to harmonize the two (LG 36).

Now insofar as they are Christians, their specific and proper activity is the *apostolate*; and it points toward, and culminates in, the sacramental life and practice of the rest of mankind. In ordinary circumstances it works something like this:

> The mission of the Church concerns the salvation of men . . . Hence the apostolate of the Church and of all her members is primarily designed to manifest Christ's message by words and deeds and to communicate His grace to the world. This work is done mainly through the ministry of the Word and of the sacraments, which are entrusted in a special way to the clergy. But the laity too have their very important roles to play. . . . A true apostle looks for opportunities to announce Christ by words addressed either to nonbelievers with a view to leading them to faith, or to believers with a view to instructing and strengthening them (AA 6).

In circumstances that are less than ordinary, the laity are obliged to somehow take on the whole function of the Church, even those activities that are properly those of the clergy:

> In exceedingly trying circumstances, the laity do what they can to take the place of priests, risking their freedom and sometimes their lives to teach Christian doctrine to those around them, to train them in a religious way of life, and . . . to lead them to receive the sacraments frequently (AA 17).

Insofar as they are citizens, by contrast, they must take part in earthly tasks and activities and respect their autonomy. (But this autonomy of the temporal realm is relative; see GS 36). What the Church offers them for this role is a faith and a charity that can make a much greater contribution toward solving the problems in the way of human progress than any external change of earthly, temporal structures.

> In the course of history, temporal things have been foully abused by serious vices. Affected by original sin, men have frequently fallen into multiple errors concerning the true God, the nature of man, and the principles of the moral law. The result has been the corruption of morals and human institutions. . . . The laity must take on the renewal of the temporal order. . . . As citizens they must cooperate with other citizens. . . . The temporal order must be renewed in such a way that, without the slightest detriment to its own proper laws, it can be brought into conformity with the higher principles of the Christian life (AA 7).

In our opinion this interpretation, however much it may be grounded on conciliar texts, really fits in with an earlier theology that has since been corrected by Vatican II. But since this Council did not and could not operate out of a totally homogeneous line of thought, it could not rule out the possibility that many conciliar passages would evince a tone, a stress, and a set of terms that were based on past habits and more classic formulations. In many circles[2] it has become common to deny importance and even existence to conciliar elements that do not jibe with classical, habitual thought and practice; or else people minimize the dogmatic importance of Vatican II. Thus the distinction between preconciliar and postconciliar elements becomes irrelevant.

B. PRACTICAL CONSEQUENCES

If we are going to clarify the different positions, then, the best approach does not seem to be by examining the frequency with which they have recourse to the Council for support. It seems better to examine their consistency in drawing practical conclusions from the above-mentioned principles. Let us see what this first outlook leads to in practice.

Firstly we find a tendency to renew the Church from within, so that it will come to be an attractive religious sign in the midst of the profane world. Hence we get a liturgical renewal that clarifies the rites and brings them closer to the faithful, but without introducing into it the secular problems of contemporary man as a decisive criterion. To take one example: the rite of baptism is revised, performed in the vernacular, explained to the faithful, and presented in a "communitarian" guise; but one continues to stress that the effective (though invisible change it causes is in the whole destiny of the infant vis-à-vis other nonbaptized people. One does not relate this change to the involvement of the community vis-à-vis God and the baptized child in connection with the crisis—be it material, social, or political—that is being lived through on the "temporal" plane.

This leads to an effort, perhaps out of all proportion, to see to it that each sacrament is properly prepared for by a dialogue *about it* between the minister and the participants.

Hence we also find a tendency to renew the Church by insisting almost exclusively on a new way of exercising authority within it. In other words, the Church is to be transformed from within into a more flexible institution where decision is always preceded by dialogue, and where the layman is always regarded and respected as an active rather than a passive member of the People of God.

Now such changes may well have great value, but that is not the point we are stressing here. What we are stressing here is that these changes stop at the doors of the Church, so to speak. The world and its earthly problems are not just kept outside—or at least that is not the main thing. Rather, the world and its problems are not seen to be the principal and authentic source of any change for a Church that is supposed to live, judge itself, and change in relation to them.

Secondly, the consequences of this first interpretation of our critical conciliar text show up in the matter of evangelization: i.e., in the activity through which the Church seeks to transmit Christ's good news to non-Christians. When the transmission of this message is mentioned in the passages quoted above, we do not find any mention of man's situation, expectations, or problems. It is as if the gospel were good news by and of itself, without any necessary reference to the concrete situation of human beings.

The texts do admit that human values are to recognized and respected. But it is not because they are the basis of a good news that would not be such without them. This recognition is required so that we can again "relate them to their divine source" (GS 11). The internal logic of this first interpretation, which is primarily interested in "religious" finality, is characterized by a preoccupation to "elevate" what it encounters. It is not its task, at least not directly, to modify or change the existing values in a human race which is often alienated and enslaved socially and politically. Consciousness-raising and evangelization are distinguished as two different tasks and, what is more, they are dissociated from one another. One leads to temporal, earthly progress; the other is aimed at the progress of the kingdom.

Thirdly, the rhythm and pace of pastoral transformation is another area in which the practical consequences of this first interpretation show up. Once we have an organized pastoral plan aimed at bringing about a gradual change in the faithful and in the activity of the Church, the next problem that comes up is the *pace* at which this change should be carried forward. Scarcely is the work of renewal initiated when we find two wings forming in the Church. One is the conservative wing. It cannot avoid accepting some change. But wielding the threat of possible schism, it forces this change to be reduced to minimal proportions, and to be inplemented at a hopelessly slow pace so that everyone can manage to adapt to it. The other wing is that of the progressives. Wielding the threat of silent apostasy in practice—i.e., indifference, aloofness—it demands that pastoral renewal proceed at the same pace as worldly problems do.

Oddly enough, the Church seems to more afraid of the possible schism than of the possible apostasy. The pace of transformation slows down so as not to leave behind Christians who still demand to practice the sacraments and belong to the Church, even when they are told that the Church is not that. But there seems to be no problem in the fact that the slow pace of progress alienates other people who are more deeply concerned by human problems, and who do not find it so difficult to stop frequenting the Church and its sacraments if they are not truly related to man's real needs in history.

But this pastoral attitude will not seem so curious if we realize that the wing which is usually victorious in this matter is the one which is disposed to keep on demanding the sacraments because it sees them as something critical and decisive. After all, when all is said and done, does this not represent a real preoccupation and concern for the kingdom, as opposed to the "naturalism" of those who relativize or minimize the supernatural "salvific" means in favor of temporal progress?

Fourthly, the practical consequences of this first interpretation and its real distinction between two finalities show up in the pastoral structure of the Church. This structure is clearly territorial. It indicates not so much a real involvement with man's real problems as the ecclesial possession of means of "salvation" that are to be distributed and brought more closely in contact with the faithful.

How true this is, especially in Latin America, can be seen from the attitude that determines how the "gaps" in a given territory are to be filled. No account is taken of the capacity of priests to make contact with the real-life problems of people living in a specific culture that is not easy to interpret. Instead one has recourse to national priests and foreign missionaries indiscriminately.[3] The general feeling is that any priest, by virtue of being a priest or having priestly powers, is useful in the area—quite apart from his understanding of Christianity, his ideas, and his involvement or noninvolvement in the problems related to the temporal progress of the country to which he has been sent.

II. One History and One Efficacy

But the conciliar text in question, which refers to the careful distinction that must be made between the growth of the kingdom and earthly progress, is open to other interpretations. This is especially clear when one realizes that Vatican II itself urges us not to turn this "distinction" into a "separation" (cf. GS 39 and 40).

Thus one can say that there is no question of a *real* distinction between two finalities here; that in the concrete history of mankind there exists only one finality—which is, of course, a supernatural one. In other words, growth of the kingdom and authentic earthly progress are to be identified with each other—both in our outlook and our activities.

What, then, is the nature of the distinction that we must be so careful to make? It is a conceptual distinction. Temporal progress is believed to be merely human and natural. But in fact the Christian knows that in this progress there exists an invisible but decisive element: the power of God is moving it along through love and is leading it inexorably to the universal triumph of love—i.e., the recapitulation of the whole universe in Christ. In knowing about "the growth of the kingdom," the Christian knows about another dimension of temporal progress that is truly present even though invisible.

A. CONCILIAR SUPPORT

We know that man does not have two vocations in history—which would be the case if the growth of the kingdom and earthly progress were really different finalities. We know that man's vocation is one and divine.

> For, since Christ died for all men, and since the ultimate vocation of man is in fact one, and divine, we ought to believe that the Holy Spirit in a manner known only to God offers to every man the possibility of being associated with this paschal mystery (GS 22).

Now it would be very difficult to reconcile these statements with the notion that the Church has some finality relating to religious salvation while secular history has some temporal, human finality. What is more, the Council also affirms that all human beings in time—that is, during their life and personal history on earth—have a vocation that does not depend on whether they have been baptized or not.

> From the very circumstance of his origin, man is already invited to converse with God (GS 22).

And the broad lines of Christian existence, viewed in historical cross-section, are identical with those of every man of good will.

> The Christian man, conformed to the likeness of that Son . . . receives "the first fruits of the Spirit" (Rom 8:23) by which he becomes capable of discharging the new law of love. Through this Spirit . . . the whole man is renewed from within, even to the achievement of "the redemption of the body." . . . Pressing upon the Christian, to be sure, are the need and the duty to battle against evil through manifold tribulations . . . But, linked with the paschal mystery and patterned on the dying Christ, he will hasten forward to resurrection in the strength which comes from hope. All this holds true not only for Christians, but for all men of good will in whose hearts grace works in an unseen way (GS 22).

On the other side of the coin we find much the same thing. When the Council describes the values that will undergo resurrection later on, they are described in terms of those values that have been won by men of good will in the course of earthly history. So is it not really a description of authentic earthly progress and its wondrous denouement?

> For after we have obeyed the Lord, and in His Spirit nurtured on earth the values of human dignity, brotherhood and freedom, and indeed all the good fruits of our nature and enterprise, we will find them again, but freed from stain, burnished and transfigured (GS 39).

> What was sown in weakness and corruption will be clothed with incorruptibility. While charity and its fruits endure, all that creation which God made on man's account will be unchained from the bondage of vanity (GS 39).

In historical events, then, the identicalness of the two finalities seems too obvious to deny in the texts just cited. By the same token, however, a distinction is evident in these texts as well. This distinction comes from that which the Christian *knows* through divine revelation. The things nurtured in earthly progress are sown "in weakness and corruption" because grace, which works in all men, works in unbelievers "in an unseen way." On the other hand, revelation uncovers the progress of the kingdom in the temporal progress of humanity. Hence it clarifies the mystery of concrete man, who is struggling in history. Thus, after affirming the identicalness of the destiny shared by the Christian and the man of good will (who is interested and involved only in earthly progress), the Council goes on to say:

> Such is the mystery of man, and it is a great one, as seen by believers in the light of Christian revelation (GS 22).

The conceptual difference, precisely because it is a difference and because it is on the conceptual level, is converted into service. It also converts the whole Church and its most specific elements into a contribution to the authentic earthly progress of the human race, not by virtue of some reflex, second-line action, but by virtue of the Church's very own nature. Thus the very nature and purpose of the sacraments (SC 62) ties them to faith:

> They not only presuppose faith, but by words and objects they also nourish, strengthen, and express it; that is why they are called "sacraments of faith" (SC 59).

Faith, in turn, has no finality in itself; nor does it have any direct efficacy bearing upon some sort of religious salvation. Rather, as the Council puts it:

> Faith throws a new light on everything, manifests God's design for man's total vocation, and thus directs the mind to solutions which are fully human (GS 11).

B. PRACTICAL CONSEQUENCES

Here again the full scope and import of this interpretation can best be seen in the practical conclusions that derive from it.

The first consequence of this interpretation is that church renewal has something outside of itself as its wellspring and measuring rod. That something is its liberative effectiveness in history—those fully human solutions that are supposed to be found for the problems of history. Hence the efficacy of the Church is measured by its effective contribution to the liberation of man, even when it is a question of the Church's most distinctive features such as faith and the sacraments. This criterion and goal, however, is exactly the same one that all men of good will seek in their commitment to the tasks of history. For those who do not have faith, these tasks are called temporal. But Christians know that they have eternal value.[4]

The second consequence is very much related to the first one. Perhaps it, more than any other, typifies this interpretation—at least on the

Latin American continent. People realize that decisive changes on behalf
of man's liberation can be effected in a short space of time, provided
that the masses are mobilized. So the Church is confronted with the
problem of making a contribution that is more hurried than profound.
Everyone knows that at certain moments in history a decision made
at the right moment can be more conclusive than a deeper process
of transformation over a long run. Well if the Church takes its mission
of service seriously, and if it accepts this calculus of historical effectiveness
which can be a "sign of the times," then one of the factors to be considered
is the historical power it still enjoys—thanks in part to the semimagical motivations that are bound up with faith and the sacraments. Its
religious authority has taken on mass dimensions that still perdure in
every realm of civic life, despite the growing process of secularization.
So the question is: Wouldn't the Church make a greater contribution
to man's liberation by using the power it still has to hurtle the masses
toward a liberation that, in terms of the Latin American situation, seems
to be opportune and timely on the political level?

And this brings us to the third consequence: evangelization and
political conscientization (or "consciousness-raising") tend to be made
identical. An organized pastoral effort, framed in this perspective, would
have to arrive quickly at the fundamental political options that really
matter. And these options would have to be shouldered by the hierarchy
in a clear, unmistakable way. In the meantime, people would read and
analyze the documents of the hierarchy to find these options, which
are often implicit in them.

Thus this outlook tends to be critical of any reform centering around
things, such as the sacraments, which do not seem to have any power
to exert a liberative impact of a decisive sort in the short run. Such
reform is written off as "internal" reform, and so it is in many cases.
And even when such reform of doctrine or the sacraments is aimed
at developing a conscious sense of liberation, the process would have
to be a long one—especially if it is expected to reach the masses, whose
strategic importance for any political change is undeniable. In such a
situation it would seem to be much better to postpone church reform,
and to use the mass-based religious exigency that already exists to extract
clearcut position-taking from the whole ambit of the Church.

Within the logic of this whole interpretation, we are not surprised
to find a prior undervaluation of the internal unfolding of the faith
and its sacramental, communitarian explication *over the long run*. There
is no hypocrisy in this. It is a matter of tactics, grounded on the same
finality that the Church recognizes as its own.

The fourth consequence of this interpretation is that the function
and the very nature of the parish are called into crisis. And the same
thing happens to the notion and function of the priest, which have
been traditionally associated with the seemingly immutable activities of
the Church and dissociated from urgent historical tasks. It is as if they

symbolize a Christianity that has lost its feel for liberation and its own role in that process.[5]

III One History and a Twofold Efficacy

There is a third possible interpretation of the conciliar text in question. In its theoretical formulation it appears to be very much like the second interpretation. But its different emphasis leads to practical conclusions and consequences of a very different sort.

Like the second interpretation, this third interpretation maintains that there is only one real finality that combines temporal progress and the growth of the kingdom into one single, supernatural destiny for man. Thus the distinction between the two is conceptual. But unlike the second interpretation, this third interpretation stresses the specific contribution that revelation about the growth of the kingdom can bring to that which, for nonbelievers, is only earthly progress.

It is not just that the Christian knows that authentic earthly progress is also progress for the kingdom, thanks to God's hidden activity. It is not just that earthly progress also shares in the certainty of the resurrection. The fact is that God's revelation in history is a factor added to the analysis of history by itself, so that we can find a broader and deeper solution to any given problem.

A. CONCILIAR SUPPORT

This third interpretation looks to the same conciliar texts for support that the second interpretation does. It is not worth repeating those texts here. The important thing is to see where this third interpretation puts the stress, and where its difference from the second interpretation crops up. This may well be evident from the central text on faith that was cited above:

> Faith throws a new light on everything . . . and thus directs the mind to solutions which are fully human (GS 11).

The second interpretation rightly sees in this passage a shift from a purely religious valuation of faith (and hence of the sacraments) to a *functional* valuation that is clearly oriented around historical problems.

Operating from this starting point, the third interpretation adds a complementary stress. It maintains that when the Council says that "faith throws a new light on everything," it is referring to much more than the simple fact of knowing through revelation what the thrust and destiny of worldly history is.

In the mind of the Council Fathers, this all-illuminating faith is not simply the result of knowing intellectually the fundamental enuntiations of the Christian message. As we see it, the Council is referring to some kind of "sixth sense," to the "prophetic" outlook that can be achieved by a Christian whose life is a long and deep interpenetration of historical analysis with an equally historical communitarian embodiment of the revealed message.

To characterize this sixth sense in theoretical terms, we would say that it is not an understanding of the extramundane, or a prefabricated formula that can be applied to history, or the result of a more profound and total analysis of purely historical data. Hence it represents a *distinctive and specific* contribution to the quest for truth that the Christian is obliged to undertake with the rest of mankind (*cf.* GS 16).

B. PRACTICAL CONSEQUENCES

The first consequence here, as in the case of the second interpretation, is that the impetus for renewal is the conviction that only one thing has value in the activity of the Church: namely, that which is *translated* and brought over to man's problems, commitments, and effective work in history.

The only thing is that in this case the work of *translation* is pictured as a long-term process and task, wherein the community establishes a much deeper fusion of the message and its historical import. It does not mean simply new motives of action and a heightened generosity in committing oneself to man's liberation—factors which could be brought about by a rapid change in people's outlook. What it entails is a work of building that will go on over a whole lifetime, as people become more and more familiar with the divine message and more and more involved in the work of history. Through reflection these two processes will become deeply fused with each other, so that one will be able to fashion a *key* which, when applied to historical analysis, will also help him to figure out the how of liberation.

As was the case with the second interpretation, this key is a useless and counterfeit element if it is not applied to history, to that for which it is destined.[6] But by the same token, if this key does not function, if history is analyzed solely with the instruments that it itself provides, then the Christian community will fail to make the contribution that is specifically its own.

Consistent with this, the second consequence is that consciousness-raising and evangelization are closely tied together but are not to be confused with each other. The function of "translating" the revealed message cannot be absorbed or taken over by the function which transforms man from a passive object to a conscious subject of history. Neither can it be detached from the latter process, for without the latter process it cannot be "good news" for man.[7] Thus the process of evangelization is inserted within the process of consciousness-raising and respects its pace. But it also adds an element which, without being ahistorical, does transcend that which comes from an understanding of the mechanisms of history.[8]

The third consequence is that it disagrees with the second interpretation on the role of the Church in this whole process. It does agree that everything in the Church, in accordance with God's plan, has meaning only to the extent that it renders service to historical progress. It also agrees that historical progress offers opportunities, meeting points, and critical urgencies—especially in the framework of present-day Latin America. But it does not agree that the Church can provide mass-directed service of the short-term variety that is now being demanded by some.

This judgment is grounded on a two-edged reason which represents the meeting point of a sociological view and a theological view. In the first place, it is our feeling that a serious political analysis of the situation would show that if our profession of faith and our sacramental practice *has not ripened* in a process of critical historical involvement, then these elements are so dependent on the status quo that they cannot be turned against it by a set of definitions from the ecclesiastical hierarchy—even supposing that these definitions were clear, unanimous, and not suspect of alien strands.

In the second place, this interpretation, which talks about the specific and distinctive contribution of a community deepening its faith on every level in order to find a key to history, cannot take an inventory of its results before it has undergone the experience itself. And undergoing this experience, with all that implies, is itself a matter of faith: of faith in the inexhaustible fecundity of the message; of faith in the community that lives this message, respecting the pace of time required for its maturation. But even then this end result, glimpsed hazily rather than clearly seen, must be taken into consideration when we are dealing with "right moments" or "critical needs" in history. Otherwise these "right moments" and "critical needs" may prove to be "false prophets" because they were unable to provide a solid basis for thoroughgoing changes. Could it be that the second interpretation, discussed above, clings to a semi-magical conception of history?

The fourth consequence derives from the recognition of the fact that it is essential for the Church to *translate* divine revelation to history. If this is so, then *two* complementary tasks become most important: (1) the divine message must be brought closer to history and its problems; (2) man's analysis of history must be brought closer to the message of divine revelation. As was the case with the second interpretation, this leads to revaluation of the central role and task of the layman. But, unlike the second interpretation, it also leads to a revaluation of the specific role and function of the priest and its attendant features: preparation, life style, requirements of time, etc. One should note, however, that this revaluation is closer in the concrete to the devaluation of the second interpretation than to the valuation put on them by the first interpretation. For the latter interpretation sees them as having direct value and efficacy for some goal of salvation that does not have to go through the test of historical effectiveness.

The first conclusion to be drawn from the preceding treatment is that there is not *one* conciliar position on the level of the Church's common praxis. Rather there are different possible interpretations and positions, and the matter is still open. It is evident that the Council was made up of persons and groups with different outlooks and theologies, and all of them left their mark on the Council.[9] Hence the Council is not and cannot be some kind of rule book that we merely have to *apply*. It leaves us with profound questions as well as profound answers. That does not mean that every interpretation of it has equal merit. The Medellín Conference felt this and, far more strongly than *Gaudium et spes,* it leaned toward the second or third interpretation described above.

The second conclusion is that, once again in the realm of real-life deeds and facts, we must determine where the tensions and problems of today's Church come to a head vis-à-vis the teachings of Vatican II. On the level of the priest, especially those priests engaged in a more mass-centered pastoral effort, the most difficult option would seem to be between the first interpretation on the one hand and the other two interpretations on the other hand. It is a matter of knowing whether the priest is or is not disposed to judge his whole pastoral effort in terms of a criterion that seems new and secular: i. e., the effective contribution of the Church to progress and liberation in history.

This set of problems, closer to priestly preoccupations and structures, is not the one that most affects lay groups that are now getting a clearer awareness of their function in the Church and its significance. With them the decisive option, often overlooked or not adverted to by pastors, is clearly between the second and the third interpretation.[10] And what is at stake here is their participation in the Church or their alienation from it.

NOTES TO APPENDIX II

1. From the standpoint of evangelization, for example, no one would think of dividing up a city of twenty thousand inhabitants into four parishes.

2. One of the most characteristic ways of rejecting the Council is to say that it was "pastoral" and not "theological." As if earlier Councils had not been pastoral. As if the teachings of *Lumen gentium* and *Gaudium et spes*, despite the absence of condemnatory canons, were not a clear and almost classic exercise of the Church's dogmatic magisterium.

3. We feel that every foreign missioner is quite as capable of making contact with the human reality of Latin America as is the native clergy—sometimes even more adept at it. On this he can then build a solid pastoral effort. But what alarms us is the fact that such capacity is not the criterion used in most cases for inviting priests to collaborate in pastoral work here. Alarmingly enough, the criterion used seems to be the distance (both in miles and in strength) that would separate the means of salvation from the people scattered around a certain territory if foreign missionaries were not used.

4. "Therefore, all 'growth in humanity' brings us closer to 'reproducing the image of the Son so that he will be the firstborn among many brothers'" (Medellín Conference, document on Education, n. 9; MED, II, 101). As we see

it, this phrase indicates that the first interpretation was positively ruled out of the thinking of the bishops gathered at Medellín.

5. *Cf.* Introduction and Chapter, IV, CLARIFICATION II.

6. *Cf.* Chapter II, CLARIFICATION I.

7. *Cf.* Medellín Conference, document on Catechesis; MED, II, 139–45.

8. The difference between that which results from historical analysis and that which is added by some divine revelation (it too working in history) might be suggested more clearly by a remark of Chesterton's. Speaking about Stevenson on one occasion, he noted that what the latter lacked and was unconsciously looking for was a religion *qua* canon. Stevenson was looking for real trust and confidence in some exterior norm. Without such a norm, sympathy for the delight of a child contemplating a dragon could eventually turn into sympathy for the delight of the dragon eating the child.

Translator's note: I have not been able to find this exact quote from Chesterton. But many of Chesterton's works are now being reprinted by Books for Libraries Press (Freeport, New York).

9. With respect to the theological criterion for preferring one interpretation to the other, see Volume II, Chapter III, CLARIFICATION V.

10. In talking about a choice or option here, we are aware of the sociological fact that the second and third interpretations do not present themselves merely as positions to choose between. There is a logic that leads one to move to the second interpretation and stop there before going on to the third. This is what we would be inclined to call a *crisis of growth*. And since it is that, one of the most urgent pastoral tasks would seem to be to offer space, time, and understanding to those who are going through it.

APPENDIX III

A Biblical Tapestry

I The Sacred in the Midst of Ancient Israel

A. IN THE DESERT

Israel is born as a nation of people during its wanderings in the desert in search of the promised land. It is the people of Yahweh en route. Yahweh is present in the midst of his people, guiding them and protecting them. His glorious presence becomes tangible to their senses. During their forty years of wandering, this pilgrim people will have a pilgrim God. Yahweh wants a travelling tent as he journeys along with them:

> Make me a sanctuary, and I will dwell among them. Make it exactly according to the design I show you. . . . Make an Ark, a chest of acacia-wood. . . . Overlay it with pure gold both inside and out. . . . Cast four gold rings for it, and fasten them to its four feet. . . . Make poles of acacia-wood and plate them with gold, and insert the poles in the rings at the sides of the Ark to lift it (Exod. 25:8–15).

In the tent of the Tabernacle and in the Ark, Yahweh will journey with his people to the promised land. He will be with them in person:

> The Lord spoke to Moses: 'Come, go up from here, you and the people you have brought up from Egypt, to the land which I swore to Abraham, Isaac, and Jacob that I would give to their posterity' . . . Moses said to the Lord, 'Thou bidst me lead this people up, but thou hast not told me whom thou wilt send with me . . . for this nation is thy own people.' The Lord answered, 'I will go with you *in person*' . . . Moses said to him, 'Indeed if thou dost not go in person, do not send us up from here; for how can it ever be known that I and thy people have found favour with thee, except by thy going with us? So shall we be distinct, I and thy people, from all the peoples on earth.' The Lord said to Moses, 'I will do this thing that you have asked' (Exod. 33:1 and 12:17).

So begin the wanderings of Israel with its God:

> Moses used to take a tent and pitch it at a distance outside the camp. He called it the Tent of the Presence, and everyone who sought the Lord would go out to the Tent of the Presence outside the camp. Whenever Moses went out to the tent, all the people would rise and stand, each at the entrance to his tent, and follow Moses with their eyes until he entered the tent. When Moses entered it, the pillar of cloud came down, and stayed at the entrance to the tent while the Lord spoke with Moses. As soon as the people saw

138

the pillar of cloud standing at the entrance to the tent, they would all prostrate themselves, every man at the entrance to his tent. The Lord would speak with Moses face to face, as one man speaks to another. Then Moses would return to the camp (Exod. 33:7–11).

The pillar of cloud was the visible sign of the presence of the divine, of Yahweh himself, in his own tent. There is where he dwelt among his people from the start of their travels:

On the day when they set up the tabernacle, that is the Tent of the Tokens, cloud covered it, and in the evening a brightness like fire appeared over it till morning. So it continued: the cloud covered it by day and a brightness like fire by night. Whenever the cloud lifted from the tent, the Israelites struck camp, and at the place where the cloud settled, there they pitched their camp. At the command of the Lord they struck camp, and at the command of the Lord they encamped again, and continued in camp as long as the cloud rested over the Tabernacle. When the cloud stayed long over the Tabernacle, the Israelites remained in attendance on the Lord and did not move on; and it was the same when the cloud continued over the Tabernacle only a few days: at the command of the Lord they remained in camp, and at the command of the Lord they struck camp (Num. 9:15–20).

It is a wondrous proximity and at the same time a wondrous figure of Yahweh's transcendence. Living in the midst of his people and sharing their triumphs and joys, Yahweh must defend himself from man's ever-present tendency to lay hands on God, to seize the divine and put it on ice for good, so that he can have peace and security:

You shall make an altar of earth for me, and you shall sacrifice on it both your whole-offerings and your shared-offerings, your sheep and your cattle. Wherever I cause my name to be invoked, I will come to you and bless you. If you make an altar of stones for me, you must not build it of hewn stones, for if you use a chisel on it, you will profane it (Exod. 20:24–25).

Here we have the first reservation against any and every temple. Yahweh wants a presence that is both transcendent and commonplace. He does not want man to fashion him into the most beautiful and grandiose figure among human figures. He wants to be at once nearer to man and farther away from him than that:

On the day when the Lord spoke to you out of the fire on Horeb, you saw no figure of any kind; so take good care not to fall into the degrading practice of making figures carved in relief, in the form of a man or a woman, or of any animal on earth or bird that flies in the air, or of any reptile on the ground or fish in the waters under the earth. Nor must you raise your eyes to the heavens and look up to the sun, the moon, and the stars, all the host of heaven, and be led on to bow down to them and worship them; the Lord your God assigned these for the worship of the various peoples under heaven (Deut. 4:15–19).

When Israel grows tired of waiting and fashions a golden calf in the Sinai desert, this is not idolatry in the current sense of the term. They are not worshipping a strange god. What it is, is stubborness. The golden calf, fashioned out of the people's gold earrings and ornaments, is the first temple built to Yahweh, in a sense:

> When the people saw that Moses was so long in coming down from the mountain, they confronted Aaron and said to him, 'Come, make us gods to go ahead of us . . . ' Aaron answered them, 'Strip the gold rings from the ears of your wives and daughters, and bring them to me' . . . He took them out of their hands, cast the metal in a mould, and made it into the image of a bull-calf. 'These', he said, 'are your gods, O Israel, that brought you up from Egypt.' Then Aaron was afraid and built an altar in front of it and issued this proclamation, 'Tomorrow there is to be a pilgrim-feast to the Lord' . . . But the Lord said to Moses, 'Go down at once, for your people, the people you brought up from Egypt, have done a disgraceful thing . . . ' So the Lord said to Moses, 'I have considered this people and I see that they are a stubborn people' (Exod. 32:1–9).

B. IN THE PROMISED LAND

Now Israel is no longer a nomadic, wayfaring people. It has a king, David, like every other king around; a capital, Jerusalem, like every other capital; and a royal palace, like every other royal palace. On the other hand, there is one anachronistic vestige of a bygone age: the God of Israel still dwells in a tent, and the Ark still bears the rings and poles that were used to transport it across the desert:

> As soon as the king was established in his house and the Lord had given him security from his enemies on all sides, he said to Nathan the prophet, 'Here I live in a house of cedar, while the Ark of God is housed in curtains.' Nathan answered the king, 'Very well, do whatever you have in mind, for the Lord is with you.' But that night the word of the Lord came to Nathan: 'Go and say to David my servant, "This is the word of the Lord: Are you the man to build me a house to dwell in? Down to this day I have never dwelt in a house since I brought Israel up from Egypt; I made my journey in a tent and a tabernacle. Wherever I journeyed with Israel, did I ever ask any of the judges . . . why they had not built me a house of cedar?" (2 Sam. 7:1–7).

Times have changed when we come to Solomon. The security and power of the Israelite nation have increased greatly. One must now associate Yahweh with the very best of both and station him in the capital of the kingdom. The divine element must be made the most glorious and effective part of the life of the nation:

> When all the work which Solomon did for the house of the Lord was completed . . . then Solomon summoned the elders of Israel, and all the heads of the tribes who were chiefs of families in Israel, to assemble in Jerusalem, in order to bring up the Ark of the Covenant of the Lord from the City of David, which is called Zion. . . . When the elders of Israel had all come, the Levites took the Ark and carried it up with the Tent of the Presence and all the sacred furnishings of the Tent. . . . There was nothing inside the Ark but the two tablets which Moses had put there at Horeb, the tablets of the covenant which the Lord made with the Israelites when they left

Egypt. . . . Now the trumpeters and the singers joined in unison to sound forth praise and thanksgiving to the Lord, and the song was raised with trumpets, cymbals, and musical instruments, in praise of the Lord, because 'that is good, for his love endures for ever'; and the house was filled with the cloud of the glory of the Lord. The priests could not continue to minister because of the cloud, for the glory of the Lord filled the house of God. Then Solomon said: "O Lord who hast chosen to dwell in thick darkness, here have I built thee a lofty house, a habitation for thee to occupy for ever" (2 Chron. 5:1–6:2).

Solomon had not comprehended Yahweh's reservations about any and every temple:

And as they stood waiting, the king turned round and blessed all the assembly of Israel in these words: 'Blessed be the Lord the God of Israel. . . . My father David had in mind to build a house in honour of the name of the Lord the God of Israel, but the Lord said to him, "You purposed to build a house in honour of my name; and your purpose was good. Nevertheless, you shall not build it; but the son who is to be born to you, he shall build the house in honour of my name." The Lord has now fulfilled his promise: I have succeeded my father David and taken his place on the throne of Israel, as the Lord promised; and I have built the house in honour of the name of the Lord the God of Israel. I have installed there the Ark containing the covenant of the Lord which he made with Israel' (2 Chron. 6:3–11).

In the eyes of Solomon, the temple is destined to be the sacred, privileged place and time in which the most serious problems of the nation will be resolved—through the divine power invoked by prayer and through the ritual sacrifice offered by priests chosen and set aside for this purpose:

Then Solomon . . . spread out his hands . . . [and] said, 'O Lord God of Israel . . . attend to the prayer and the supplication of thy servant . . . that thine eyes may ever be upon this house day and night, this place of which thou didst say, "It shall receive my Name" . . . Hear thou the supplications of thy servant and thy people Israel when they pray towards this place. . . . When a man wrongs his neighbour and he is adjured to take an oath, and the adjuration is made before thy altar in this house, then do thou hear from heaven. . . . When thy people Israel are defeated by an enemy because they have sinned against thee, and they turn back to thee . . . do thou hear from heaven' . . . When the heavens are shut up and there is no rain, because thy servant and thy people Israel have sinned against thee, and when they pray towards this place . . . do thou hear from heaven. . . . If there is famine in the land . . . then hear the prayer or supplication of every man among thy people Israel. . . . The foreigner too, the man who has come from a distant land . . . when he comes and prays towards this house, hear from heaven. . . . When thy people go to war with their enemies . . . do thou from heaven hear their prayer and supplication. . . . Should they sin against thee . . . then from thy dwelling do thou hear their prayer and supplications. . . . Now, O my God, let thine eyes be open and thy ears attentive to the prayer made in this place. Arise now, O Lord God, and come to thy place of rest, thou and the Ark of thy might' (2 Chron. 6:13–41).

Yahweh accepts the trusting plea of his people, but he warns about having any false sense of security. The temple they now have, with all its grandeur, is just as fragile as the ancient tent if someone thinks he can lay hands on it and use it for his own ends:

> When Solomon had finished this prayer, fire came down from heaven and consumed the whole-offering and the sacrifices, while the glory of the Lord filled the house. The priests were unable to enter the house of the Lord because the glory of the Lord had filled it. All the Israelites were watching as the fire came down with the glory of the Lord on the house, and where they stood on the paved court they bowed low to the ground and worshipped and gave thanks to the Lord, because 'that is good, for his love endures for ever.' Then the king and all the people offered sacrifice before the Lord. King Solomon offered a sacrifice of twenty-two thousand oxen and a hundred and twenty sheep; in this way the king and all the people dedicated the house of God. . . . When Solomon had finished the house of the Lord and the royal palace and had successfully carried out all that he had planned for the house of the Lord and the palace, the Lord appeared to him by night and said, 'I have heard your prayer and I have chosen this place to be my place of sacrifice. When I shut up the heavens and there is no rain, or command the locusts to consume the land, or send a pestilence against my people, if my people whom I have named my own submit and pray to me and seek me and turn back from their evil ways, I will hear from heaven and forgive their sins and heal their land. Now my eyes will be open and my ears attentive to the prayers which are made in this place. I have chosen and consecrated this house, that my Name may be there for all time and my eyes and my heart be fixed on it for ever. . . . But if you turn away and forsake my statutes and my commandments which I have set before you, and if you go and serve other gods and prostrate yourselves before them, then I will uproot you from my land which I gave you, I will reject this house which I have consecrated in honour of my name, and make it a byword and an object-lesson among all peoples' (2 Chron. 7:1–4,11–20).

C. IN THE EXILE

Yahweh's warnings prove to be right. The temple ends up by falsifying Yahweh's presence among his people. Over the course of several centuries prophets will be sent to tell Israel that Yahweh's true presence is something else; that he is present when and where righteousness is present, not in some place or time set apart:

> Wait, says the Lord, the days are coming when I will bestow on Israel and Judah all the blessings I have promised them. In those days, at that time, I will make a righteous Branch of David spring up; he shall maintain law and justice in the land. In those days Judah shall be kept safe and Jerusalem shall live undisturbed; and this shall be her name: The Lord is our Righteousness (Jer. 33:14–16).

Thus the preaching of the prophets clearly replaces the sacred realm of the temple with the city and the day-by-day life of the people:

> Loyalty is my desire, not sacrifice; not whole-offerings but the knowledge of God (Hos. 6:6).

This is the point that Isaiah develops right at the very start of his preaching:

> Hear the word of the Lord, you rulers of Sodom; attend, you people of Gomorrah, to the instruction of our God: Your countless sacrifices, what are they to me? says the Lord. I am sated with whole-offerings of rams and the fat of buffaloes. . . . I cannot tolerate your new moons and your festivals; they have become a burden to me, and I can put up with them no longer. When you lift your hands outspread in prayer, I will hide my eyes from you. Though you offer countless prayers I will not listen. There is blood on your hands; wash yourselves and be clean. Put away the evil of your deeds, away out of my sight. Cease to do evil and learn to do right, pursue justice and champion the oppressed; give the orphan his rights, plead the widow's cause (Isa. 1:10–17).

The temple has been turned into the direct negation of Yahweh's presence among his people:

> Stand at the gate of the Lord's house and there make your proclamation: Listen to the words of the Lord, all you men of Judah who come in through these gates to worship him. These are the words of the Lord of Hosts the God of Israel: Mend your ways and your doings, that I may let you live in this place. You keep saying, 'This place is the temple of the Lord, the temple of the Lord, the temple of the Lord!' This catchword of yours is a lie; put no trust in it. Mend your ways and your doings, deal fairly with one another, do not oppress the alien, the orphan, and the widow, shed no innocent blood in this place, do not run after other gods to your own ruin. Then will I let you live in this place, in the land which I gave long ago to your forefathers for all time. You gain nothing by putting your trust in this lie. You steal, you murder, you commit adultery and perjury, you burn sacrifices to Baal, you run after other gods whom you have not known; then you come and stand before me in this house, which bears my name, and say, 'We are safe'; safe, you think, to indulge in all these abominations. Do you think that this house, this house which bears my name, is a robbers' cave? I myself have seen all this, says the Lord. Go to my shrine at Shiloh, which once I made a dwelling for my Name, and see what I did to it because of the wickedness of my people Israel (Jer. 7:2–12).

The same opposition between false proximity to God and real closeness, between his authentic presence and a counterfeit presence, is marked by Isaiah:

> Call my people to account for their transgression and the house of Jacob for their sins, although they ask counsel of me day by day and say they delight in knowing my ways, although, like nations which have acted rightly and not forsaken the just law of their gods, they ask me for righteous laws and say they delight in approaching God. Why do we fast, if thou dost not see it? Why mortify ourselves, if thou payest no heed? Since you serve your own interest only on your fast-day and make all your men work the harder, since your fasting leads only to wrangling and strife and dealing vicious blows with the fist, on such a day you are keeping no fast that will carry your cry to heaven. . . . Is not this what I require of you as a fast: to loose the fetters of injustice, to untie the knots of the yoke, to snap every yoke and set free those who have been crushed? Is it not sharing your

food with the hungry, taking the homeless poor into your house, clothing
the naked when you meet them and never evading a duty to your kinsfolk?
Then shall your light break forth like the dawn and soon you will grow
healthy like a wound newly healed; your own righteousness shall be your
vanguard and the glory of the Lord your rearguard (Isa. 58:1–8).

In this image of a journey where Yahweh (i.e., your own righteousness)
takes up the rearguard and the vanguard, we have a clear picture of
the journey of wayfaring Israel and Yahweh's authentic presence among
his people. Nostalgia for that earlier presence of Yahweh among his
people, as opposed to the ambiguity of the temple, is also present in
the overall context of the earlier citation from Jeremiah:

> These are the words of the Lord of Hosts the God of Israel: Add whole-
> offerings to sacrifices and eat the flesh if you will. But when I brought
> your forefathers out of Egypt, I gave them no commands about whole-
> offering and sacrifice; I said not a word about them. What I did command
> them was this: If you obey me, I will be your God and you shall be my
> people. You must conform to all my commands, if you would prosper (Jer.
> 7:21–23).

The same opposition shows up in Amos:

> For all this, because you levy taxes on the poor and extort a tribute of
> grain from them, though you have built houses of hewn stone, you shall
> not live in them, though you have planted pleasant vineyards, you shall
> not drink wine from them. For I know how many your crimes are and
> how countless your sins. . . . I hate, I spurn your pilgrim-feasts; I will not
> delight in your sacred ceremonies. . . . Spare me the sound of your songs;
> I cannot endure the music of your lutes. Let justice roll on like a river
> and righteousness like an ever-flowing stream. Did you bring me sacrifices
> and gifts, you people of Israel, those forty years in the wilderness? (Amos.
> 5:11–12; 21–25).

Gradually an explanation dawns, and the consequences are drawn. The
explanation is that Israel is no longer the wayfaring Israel of old with
its wayfarer religion. It is an established nation with an established,
self-satisfied religion:

> But I have been the Lord your God since your days in Egypt, when you
> knew no other saviour than me, no god but me. I cared for you in the
> wilderness, in a land of burning heat, as if you were in pasture. So they
> were filled, and, being filled, grew proud; and so they forgot me (Hos.
> 13:4–6).

The consequence of this fact is clear. Hosea describes it within the
framework of his imagery: i.e., the marriage between Yahweh and Israel:

> I will woo her, I will go with her into the wilderness and comfort her . . . and
> there she will answer as in her youth, when she came up out of Egypt
> (Hos. 2:14–15).

In this great purification process, from which a loyal remnant will emerge, false confidence in the temple will be replaced by an authentic spiritual poverty that is now absent in self-satisfied Israel:

> On that day, Jerusalem, you shall not be put to shame for all your deeds by which you have rebelled against me; for then I will rid you of your proud and arrogant citizens, and never again shall you flaunt your pride on my holy hill. But I will leave in you a people afflicted and poor. The survivors in Israel shall find refuge in the name of the Lord; they shall no longer do wrong (Zeph. 3:11–13).

So that vainglorious boasting will be erased completely, the glory of God (i.e., the divine presence) will abandon the temple and once again will follow the exiles without a roof over its head on this earth:

> While I was prophesying, Pelatiah son of Benaiah fell dead; and I threw myself upon my face, crying aloud, 'O Lord God, must thou make an end of all the Israelites who are left?' The word of the Lord came to me: Man, they are your brothers, your brothers and your kinsmen, this whole people of Israel, to whom the men who now live in Jerusalem have said, 'Keep your distance from the Lord; the land has been made over to us as our property.' Say therefore, These are the words of the Lord God: When I sent them far away among the nations and scattered them in many lands, for a while *I became their sanctuary* in the countries to which they had gone. Say therefore, These are the words of the Lord God: I will gather them from among the nations and assemble them from the countries over which I have scattered them, and I will give them the soil of Israel . . . I will give them a different heart and put a new spirit into them; I will take the heart of stone out of their bodies and give them a heart of flesh. Then they will conform to my statutes and keep my laws. They will become my people, and I will become their God. . . . Then the cherubim lifted their wings, with the wheels beside them and the glory of the God of Israel above them. The glory of the Lord rose up and left the city, and halted on the mountain to the east of it (Ezek. 11:13–24).

D. IN THE RESTORATION

This prophetic teaching did little good. When Yahweh brings his people back from exile, Haggai feels that the religious life of the people must be centered once again around and in the reconstructed temple. There, he feels, is the one and only presence of Yahweh:

> These are the words of the Lord of Hosts: This nation says to itself that it is not yet time for the house of the Lord to be rebuilt. Then this word came through Haggai the prophet: Is it a time for you to live in your own well-roofed houses, while this house lies in ruins? Now these are the words of the Lord of Hosts: Consider your way of life. You have sown much but reaped little; you eat but never as much as you wish, you drink but never more than you need, you are clothed but never warm, and the labourer puts his wages into a purse with a hole in it. These are the words of the Lord of Hosts: Consider your way of life. Go up into the hills, fetch timber, and build a house acceptable to me, where I can show my glory, says the

Lord. You look for much and get little. At the moment when you would bring home the harvest, I blast it. Why? says the Lord of Hosts. Because my house lies in ruins, while each of you has a house that he can run to (Hag. 1:2–9).

The lesson of David and of the desert seems to be forgotten. It looks as if Yahweh wants the best of everything in Israel to affirm and adorn his presence:

And the rest of the people listened to what the Lord their God had said. . . . So Haggai the Lord's messenger, as the Lord had commissioned him, said to the people: I am with you, says the Lord. . . . I will fill this house with glory. . . . Mine is the silver and mine the gold, says the Lord of Hosts, and the glory of this latter house shall surpass the glory of the former. . . . In this place will I grant prosperity and peace. This is the very word of the Lord of Hosts (Hag. 1:12–13; 2:7–9).

Israel, now a subject nation and without any evident historical mission, spiritualizes her religion and centers it on this edifice where the glory of Yahweh resides: i.e., the temple:

As a hind longs for the running streams, so do I long for thee, O God. With my whole being I thirst for God, the living God. When shall I come to God and appear in his presence? Day and night, tears are my food; 'Where is your God?' they ask me all day long. As I pour out my soul in distress, I call to mind how I marched in the ranks of the great to the house of God, among exultant shouts of praise, the clamour of the pilgrims. . . . Send forth thy light and thy truth to be my guide and lead me to thy holy hill, to thy tabernacle, then shall I come to the altar of God, the God of my joy, and praise thee on the harp, O God, thou God of my delight (Ps. 42:1–4; 43:3–4).

How dear is thy dwelling-place, thou Lord of Hosts. I pine, I faint with longing for the courts of the Lord's temple; my whole being cries out with joy to the living God. Even the sparrow finds a home, and the swallow has her nest, where she rears her brood beside thy altars, O Lord of Hosts, my King and my God. Happy are those who dwell in thy house; they never cease from praising thee. Happy the men whose refuge is in thee, whose hearts are set on the pilgrim ways. As they pass through the thirsty valley they find water from a spring; and the Lord provides even men who lose their way with pools to quench their thirst. So they pass on from outer wall to inner, and the God of gods shows himself in Zion. . . . Better one day in thy courts than a thousand days at home (Ps. 84:1–10).

This is the religious reality that Christ encounters. What will the good news have to say about God's presence on man's earth?

II The Sacred in the New Israel

A. COSMIC PERSPECTIVES

In the perspective of the New Testament, the three decisive cosmic moments or events (incarnation, redemption, parousia) have a relationship to the temple: i.e., to the glorious presence of God amid his people.

In the Prologue to his Gospel, John presents the journey of the Word as a descent from the Father to earth and an ascent from earth to the Father. At the apex is the incarnation:

> So the Word became flesh; he came to dwell among us, and we saw his glory, such glory as befits the Father's only Son, full of grace and truth (John 1:14).

The Gospel of Matthew makes a succinct but revealing remark when it talks about the mystery of salvation that was effected by Jesus' death and resurrection:

> Jesus again gave a loud cry, and breathed his last. At that moment the curtain of the temple was torn in two from top to bottom (Matt. 27:50–51).

The figure is being replaced by the reality, the old covenant by the new, the ancient temple by another temple that is not fashioned by human hands. That is what the Epistle to the Hebrews tells us:

> The first covenant indeed had its ordinances of divine service and its sanctuary, but a material sanctuary. For a tent was prepared—the first tent—in which was the lamp-stand, and the table with the bread of the Presence; this is called the Holy Place. Beyond the second curtain was the tent called the Most Holy Place. Here was a golden altar of incense, and the ark of the covenant plated all over with gold . . . and the tablets of the covenant; and above it the cherubim of God's glory. . . . Under this arrangement, the priests are always entering the first tent in the discharge of their duties; but the second is entered only once a year, and by the high priest alone, and even then he must take with him the blood which he offers on his own behalf and for the people's sins of ignorance. By this the Holy Spirit signifies that so long as the earlier tent still stands, the way into the sanctuary remains unrevealed. All this is symbolic, pointing to the present time. . . . But now Christ has come, high priest of good things already in being. The tent of his priesthood is a greater and more perfect one, not made by men's hands, that is, not belonging to this created world; the blood of his sacrifice is his own blood, not the blood of goats and calves; and thus he has entered the sanctuary once and for all and secured an eternal deliverance. . . . He offered himself without blemish to God, a spiritual and eternal sacrifice; and his blood will cleanse our conscience from the deadness of our former ways and fit us for the service of the living God (Heb. 9:1–14).

Finally, there is the second coming of Christ, the parousia, the inauguration of the new heavens and the new earth, the arrival of the definitive reality that has already begun on our earth. It is the manifest and complete realization of this new presence of the sacred in the midst of the human:

> Then I saw a new Jerusalem, coming down out of heaven from God. . . . I heard a loud voice proclaiming from the throne: 'Now at last God has his dwelling among men! He will dwell among them and they shall be his people, and God himself will be with them. He will wipe every tear from their eyes; there shall be an end to death, and to mourning and crying and pain; for the old order has passed away!' . . . Then one of the seven angels . . . in

the Spirit . . . carried me away to a great high mountain, and showed me
the holy city of Jerusalem coming down out of heaven from God. It shone
with the glory of God. . . . I saw no temple in the city; for its temple was
the sovereign Lord God and the Lamb. And the city had no need of sun
or moon to shine upon it; for the glory of God gave it light, and its lamp
was the Lamb. By its light shall the nations walk, and the kings of the earth
shall bring into it all their splendour. The gates of the city shall never be
shut by day—and there will be no night. The wealth and splendour of the
nations shall be brought into it; but nothing unclean shall enter nor anyone
whose ways are false (Rev. 21:1–27).

B. THE NEW BEGINNING OF THE SACRED

In a dialogue between Jesus and a Samaritan woman, which is sometimes referred to as "the book of new beginnings," we find the proclamation of a new beginning for the presence of God on earth and for
the worship that man must render to it:

Jesus said, 'Everyone who drinks this water will be thirsty again, but whoever
drinks the water that I shall give him will be an inner spring always welling
up for eternal life' . . . She replied, 'I can see that you are a prophet. Our
fathers worshipped on this mountain, but you Jews say that the temple
where God should be worshipped is in Jerusalem.' 'Believe me,' said Jesus,
'the time is coming when you will worship the Father neither on this
mountain, nor in Jerusalem. You Samaritans worship without knowing
what you worship, while we worship what we know. It is from the Jews
that salvation comes. But the time approaches, indeed it is already here,
when those who are real worshippers will worship the Father in spirit
and in truth. Such are the worshippers whom the Father wants. God is
spirit, and those who worship him must worship in spirit and in truth
(John 4:13–24).

So we have a new spiritual cult to replace the old, and a new spiritual
temple where man will worship the Father in truth. But of what exactly
does this new reality consist? As we read earlier, the Epistle to the Hebrews
tells us about the replacement of the old temple. It also tells us the
principal feature involved in this replacement: we are now dealing with
a sacred that is operative once and for all:

For Christ has entered, not that sanctuary made by men's hands which is
only a symbol of the reality, but heaven itself, to appear now before God
on our behalf. Nor is he there to offer himself again and again, as the
high priest enters the sanctuary year by year with blood not his own. If
that were so, he would have had to suffer many times since the world was
made. But as it is, he has appeared once and for all at the climax of history
to abolish sin by the sacrifice of himself. . . . Every priest stands performing
his service daily and offering time after time the same sacrifices, which can
never remove sins. But Christ offered for all time one sacrifice for sins,
and took his seat at the right hand of God, where he waits henceforth until
his enemies are made his footstool. For by one offering he has perfected
for all time those who are thus consecrated. Here we have also the testimony
of the Holy Spirit: he first says, 'This is the covenant which I will make

with them after those days, says the Lord: I will set my laws in their hearts
and write them on their understanding'; then he adds, 'and their sins and
wicked deeds I will remember no more at all.' And where these have been
forgiven, there are offerings for sin no longer (Heb. 9:24–26; 10:11–18).

So the Christian does not approach the sacred in order to lay hold
of something—he already has it once and for all. The Church at Corinth,
for example, must learn that baptism is not some sacred tool placed
above man, something that has greater or lesser efficacy depending
on the apostle who confers it:

> I have been told . . . by Chloe's people that there are quarrels among you.
> What I mean is this: each of you is saying, 'I am Paul's man', or 'I am
> for Apollos'; 'I follow Cephas', or 'I am Christ's' . . . Thank God, I never
> baptized one of you—except Crispus and Gaius. So no one can say you
> were baptized in my name (1 Cor. 1:11–12 and 14).

There is now a general principle that applies both to the profane and
the sacred realm. It allows us to comprehend the newness of Christ
and ensures that "the fact of Christ on his cross might have its full
weight" (1 Cor. 1:17). The principle is that everything has been made
subject to man and placed at his disposal:

> Everything belongs to you—Paul, Apollos, and Cephas, the world, life, and
> death, the present and the future, all of them belong to you—yet you belong
> to Christ, and Christ to God (1 Cor. 3:21–23).

The sacred is not a medium superior to man, through which man draws
closer to God. It is an interior power that transforms our present-day
activity into an imperishable creation—the true temple of God which,
as we have seen, is the new heaven and the new earth:

> We are God's fellow-workers; and you are God's garden. Or again, you are
> God's building. I am like a skilled master-builder who by God's grace laid the
> foundation, and someone else is putting up the building. Let each take care
> how he builds . . . If anyone builds on that foundation with gold, silver, and
> fine stone, or with wood, hay, and straw, the work that each man does will at
> last be brought to light; the day of judgement will expose it. For that day
> dawns in fire, and the fire will test the worth of each man's work. If a man's
> building stands, he will be rewarded; if it burns, he will have to bear the loss
> (1 Cor. 3:9–15).

To comprehend and appreciate the divine quality that gives solidity
and consistency to man's creative building (i.e., to history), we must
understand what exactly goes to make up the glory of God that filled
the temple in the Old Testament and transformed it into the divine
locus *par excellence*, the tangible manifestation of the divine presence.
Now in the Prologue of his Gospel, John tells us that the Word came
to dwell among us in the flesh and that he "saw his glory" (John 1:14).
John himself saw God's glory among us, even as the ancient Israelites
did in the desert. So the question is: When did John see the glory of
the Word that manifested his divinity?

> It was before the Passover festival. Jesus knew that his hour had come and
> he must leave this world and go to the Father. He had always loved his
> own who were in the world, and now he was to show the full extent of
> his love. . . . During supper, Jesus, well aware that the Father had entrusted
> everything to him, and that he had come from God and was going back
> to God, rose from table, laid aside his garments, and taking a towel, tied
> it round him. Then he poured water into a basin, and began to wash his
> disciples' feet and to wipe them with the towel. . . . Jesus said, 'Now the
> Son of Man is glorified, and in him God is glorified' (John 13:1-5, 31).

For John the glory of God, the visible sign of his presence among men,
was the manifestation of his boundless love and his total self-surrender.
And since this life has passed to us through our love-inspired work
of building, Paul can say that we ourselves are "God's temple" (1
Cor. 3:16). In the new Israel God is not present in some sacred place
or time. He has established his dwelling among us in the fullest sense:
i.e., we run into him every day at all hours and everywhere. He has
pinpointed the locale of this encounter. It is his presence in every human
being who needs our love:

> Then the righteous will reply, "Lord, when was it that we saw you hungry
> and fed you, or thirsty and gave you drink, a stranger and took you home,
> or naked and clothed you? When did we see you ill or in prison, and come
> to visit you?" And the king will answer, "I tell you this; anything you did
> for one of my brothers here, however humble, you did for me"
> (Matt. 25:37-40).[41]

It is logical that when this reality is revealed in all its plenitude, no
temple will exist. For God himself, present in his brothers and built
up by the history of all his brothers, will be the temple of the new
reality—the latter being both heaven and earth at once.

APPENDIX IV

Springboard Questions

As we pointed out in the first volume of this series, we found it absolutely necessary to prepare questions for the discussion periods that were an integral part of our seminars. Only in this way were the participants able to engage in probing discussions that took a hard look at accustomed images and concepts.

The questions were not meant to encourage passivity on the part of the participants. Their purpose was not to get the participants merely to "recall" or "review" what had been said in lectures or readings. They were meant to broaden the outlook of the participants by getting them to think out the logic of what they had heard and read in terms of real-life situations and problems. In short, they were meant to produce a confrontation between real life and what the participants believed they knew.

We felt that our readers might like to see the type of question we proposed and the rationale behind it. So here we offer some of the questions we proposed in connection with each chapter topic, together with an explanation accounting for our choice of these questions.

Chapter One

QUESTIONS

a) How would you account for the existence of sacraments in a process of evangelization that was being aimed at nonbelievers? In other words, how would you present them as "good news"?

b) How would you introduce the theme of sacramental practice to a Christian separated from the Church?

EXPLANATION

The aim of both questions is to focus attention on what really gives meaning to the sacraments, to move people away from the usual explanation, which presents the sacraments as a restrictive, relatively painful condition for attaining personal salvation as an individual. If the respondent has understood the chapter, he or she will realize that the quality of "good news" cannot be attributed to the sacraments directly in themselves; that first we must invert the current order of means and ends. This is a good way of finding out to what extent this inversion has been achieved in the respondent's outlook, to what extent he now realizes that the Church has not been made for the sacraments but rather that the sacraments are made for a Church sent out to the rest of humanity. It would be evident that the respondent had not understood the chapter fully if, for example, he simply said that the importance of the sacraments has been exaggerated.

Chapter Two

QUESTION

What (supernatural) effect would the following have: (1) sacraments whose signification was not understood but which were received out of obedience to God who commands their reception; (2) sacraments (?) that were perfectly understood, but that were administered by someone who was not ordained for that?

EXPLANATION

The general aim of both questions is to facilitate an understanding of sacramental efficacy. Case one is a very real one. It is the case of countless people who receive the sacraments as rites ordained by God but who do not comprehend them as signs. If the respondent answers "no effect" to Case One, this would indicate that in stressing the fact that the sacraments are signs he has lost sight of the grace that they confer. If the latter reality is kept in mind, then the response should take into account the grace conferred by virtue of the good will in every sincere person. If that is done, then the question breaks up into two questions: The first is: How do we characterize the grace received by virtue of good will alone, without the feature of signification? We want to know if the respondent will arrive at the conclusion that it is grace but not "Christian" grace, the latter being the grace which, in the plan of God, is designed to fashion the Church and prepare her for her specific mission. The second question is: Can the mere fact of obeying a religious prescription by itself be identified with "good will"? This question will indicate to what extent the respondent has grasped the importance of love-based motivation as an essential component of good will.

Case Two is also a very real one, though less frequent than Case One. One example would be certain ecumenical celebrations of the Lord's Supper at which the priest will often tell Catholics that he is participating in the role of spectator rather than in his role as a priest. What is lacking in this remembrance of the Eucharist—which is properly understood—to keep it from really being the Eucharist? People's answers to this question will show whether they see its minister as someone endowed with magical powers or as someone who presides over the formation of a community with one and the same faith. If the respondents stress the element of faith as decisive in determining whether it is a Eucharist or not, and if they see faith precisely as a communitarian bond rather than as a mere legal requisite, then they will have understood this chapter properly.

QUESTION

Someone may say: "I am going to give up the sacraments until I figure out what meaning they have." What do you think of this attitude? Is something being lost? Is it dangerous?

EXPLANATION

This question is very topical in today's Church. It forces the respondent to spell out what attitude should be taken toward the transition from rite to sign—a transition that usually does not take place in the twinkling of an eye. The answer will indicate to what extent one is prepared to value this attitude and go along with it. Or, on the other hand, it will show to what extent one still holds on to semimagical attitudes that fail to regard the needs and time-requirements involved in arriving at the truth and that only value minimal participation in the sacramental Church.

Chapter Three

QUESTION

Why do people say that baptism is a "necessity of means"—that is, an absolute necessity—for salvation?

EXPLANATION

The question seeks to resolve a language problem that is prevalent among the faithful. In speaking of the necessity of *grace,* theology has habitually referred to grace by using *the name of the sacrament* which confers this grace on Christians. Hence the necessity of grace has been confused with the necessity of its *external sign*. As a result, erroneous conclusions have been drawn in dealing with non-Christians and even in conceiving the function of the Church itself. If this linguistic problem is not resolved, current theology could nullify everything we have seen in the foregoing chapters.

QUESTION

What other key moments in man's socio-cultural existence would merit signification of God's grace therein, so that they could be experienced in a Christian, communitarian way? Would celebrating them in the liturgy turn them into sacraments too?

EXPLANATION

The question measures the degree of liberty and creativity that the Christian respondent attributes to the Church. It also measures how necessary he feels it is for Christianity to be lived with words and gestures that involve us in the major new problems faced by each new generation of human beings. An example for today, one unknown at the time of Jesus, would be the person's first involvement in political life.

Chapter Four

QUESTION

Does it make sense to practice the Eucharist where no real Christian community exists, or where there is no concrete relationship between the distribution of the sacrament and the problems of the poor, the hungry, and the exploited? Should one keep receiving communion as an individual so long as things do not change?

EXPLANATION

The case is so real that it requires little explanation. Some respondents might stress the fact that it is possible to go beyond the local "community" and commune in and with the universal Church, so to speak. A more interesting conclusion might be that the Eucharist presupposes an individual effort to create a real Christian community even though the sacraments cannot yet be celebrated *in* it.

QUESTION

Do you feel that the priest ordinarily has spare time, and that his office is therefore compatible with a secular occupation?

EXPLANATION

This timely question will show what image the respondents have of the priestly function. This in turn will enable one to situate it within the second or third interpretation we discussed in Appendix II. The point is whether or not they regard a long and thoroughgoing preparation of the Christian community in the faith as a key to history which does not come from history itself. Insofar as the priestly function is conceived in these terms, the question will show to what extent lay people recognize the concrete demands of this function and are willing to support it spiritually and materially.